In a world obsessed by *power*, I'm more interested in *authority*, because power is usually out front, while real authority is behind the scenes, almost invisible. And when I think of authority, I often think of Joni Parsley. She's been an incredible source of strength for her husband, who was literally a pioneer in developing one of the first megachurches and then a national media ministry. And she's been the center of a great family who raised a son with Asperger's syndrome. *Tapestry of Faith* is the account of that journey, and it's a powerful story of perseverance, inspiration, and hope. Whatever challenges you've encountered in your life, Joni's book is a road map to the other side.

—PHIL COOKE, PhD
FILMMAKER, MEDIA CONSULTANT, AND AUTHOR OF *ONE BIG THING: DISCOVERING WHAT YOU WERE BORN TO DO*

Tapestry of Faith is Joni Parsley's faith journal guaranteed to make you smile, chuckle, and then really laugh. It can also make you cry. You will find yourself nodding your head in agreement and maybe even shouting a passionate "Amen!" Joni Parsley in her inimitable style of delivering truth often infused with humor draws upon her own experiences and life lessons to weave a beautiful picture of the goodness and faithfulness of God, who is the centerpiece of her story. She flawlessly delves into the heart of every matter and brings to you what's important and what really matters, and she helps you to see what it is all about. She is so relatable. You will want to read *Tapestry of Faith*; it is engaging, inspiring, candid, and refreshing.

—JONI LAMB
VICE PRESIDENT, DAYSTAR NETWORK

A tapestry is the metaphorical image most appropriately used to describe this superbly written muse concerning the intricacies and complexities of life. Joni has masterfully combined random stories as well as sequenced events to make us see the beauty and awe inherent in life and living. Her unique perspective held me spellbound. It is both hilarious and thought provoking; serious but lighthearted. As I read this book, her graphic descriptions made me feel as if I was watching a blockbuster motion picture. This book is simply brilliant.

—Dr. N. Cindy Trimm
Best-selling author, life strategist,
minister of the gospel
CindyTrimm.com
Trimminternational.com

As you read *Tapestry of Faith*, you feel as though you have walked this journey with Joni Parsley. Her stories are filled with passion, love, and inspiration. At moments I laughed, and other moments my eyes welled up with tears as I felt her sincerity and heartfelt emotion in every page.

This phenomenal book is so much more than words on a page. It is a mirror that allows you to see inside yourself. As you read through these experiences and candid thoughts, you are sure to find yourself in the pages of this book. I know I did—time and time again. They take you on a journey that shows us not only what life can unexpectedly throw our way but also how our amazing God uses every piece to create the masterpiece that is you.

Tapestry of Faith is the story of life. It's moving, it's emotional, and it's REAL!

—Darlene Bishop
Darlene Bishop Ministries
www.darlenebishop.org

Joni Parsley is a longtime friend whose ministry I have enjoyed and valued through the years as we have had some parallel experiences. Her new book, *Tapestry of Faith*, is an open, honest, and inspirational account of one woman's faith in God and how that faith has sustained her through life's trials and triumphs. Her uplifting, easy-to-digest writing style will lift your spirit and give you the tools to overcome. I am happy to recommend this book to you, your church, or your organization.

—Kellie Copeland Swisher
Senior executive, Kenneth Copeland Ministries
Cofounder, Swisher Evangelistic Association, Inc.

FUNNY! No, wait…*HILARIOUS* describes Joni Parsley's book Tapestry of Faith! It just pulls you right on in! A magnetic read? Absolutely! Once you pick up this book, you will not want to put it down. Seriously, it's so relatable, so enjoyable, so inspiring, so filled with love. It's a beautiful reminder of how the Father uses everyday life to impart life lessons to us revealing His character and faithfulness. It gives me great joy to recommend this book; I know it will bless your life!

—Dr. Medina Pullings
Pastor, United Nations Church International
www.unitednationchurch.org
www.medinapullings.com

JONI PARSLEY

CHARISMA
HOUSE

Tapestry of Faith by Joni Parsley
Published by Charisma House
Charisma Media/Charisma House Book Group
600 Rinehart Road
Lake Mary, Florida 32746
www.charismahouse.com

Cover design by Justin Evans
Design Director: Bill Johnson

Visit the author's website at http://joniparsley.com.

Library of Congress Cataloging-in-Publication Data:

Parsley, Joni.
  Tapestry of faith : discovering God's beautiful design in the laughter, tears, and struggles of life / Joni Parsley.
      pages cm
  Includes bibliographical references.
  Summary: "With honesty, humor, and strength Joni Parsley walks readers through the ups and downs of her life, inspiring them to "get real with God and with others and live with

faith." The Christian life is not easy, and being a pastor's wife doesn't earn one extra credit. Daily life is mundane, stressful, joyous, and painful, and sometimes simply can't be explained. Joni Parsley's days find her facing many of the same issues that we all face. In this book she writes about and through life's challenges to weave an emotional tapestry layered with laughter, tears, questions, thoughts, errors, and struggles. With a conversational style full of engaging stories and enlightening metaphors, she demonstrates how readers can live a life of joy and faith as they:

Summary: "With honesty, humor, and strength, Joni Parsley walks readers through the ups and downs of her life--and life in general--inspiring them to get real with God and others, and live with faith"-- Provided by publisher.

ISBN 978-1-62136-516-7 (paperback) -- ISBN 978-1-62136-517-4 (ebook)

1. Parsley, Joni. 2. Christian biography--United States. I. Title.

BR1725.P2655A3 2014

289.9'4092--dc23

[B]

20130416

While the author has made every effort to provide accurate telephone numbers and Internet addresses at the time of publication, neither the publisher nor the author assumes any responsibility for errors or for changes that occur after publication.

First edition

14 15 16 17 18 — 987654321
Printed in the United States of America

To my amazing children, Ashton Blaire and Austin Chandler:

How do you describe this love that makes you breathe yet makes you breathless at the same time?

My life has been a tapestry of rich and royal hue,
An everlasting vision of the ever-changing view
A wondrous woven magic in bits of blue and gold
A tapestry to feel and see, impossible to hold.[1]

CONTENTS

FOREWORD

I BELIEVE THAT YOU never really get to know someone until you travel together. This is why I've agreed to write this foreword. Joni Askoff Parsley and I have traveled a thousand earthly journeys together as well as the far greater journey of a lifetime (greater than half of our years on this planet). *I know her*, and she knows me in a God-ordained, magnificently singular way. We two, yet one, are joined by the singular thread of true companionship. When God said, "And Adam knew Eve," there was much more than the typical connotation—He was speaking of those secrets that only our pristine parents could share, experiences, discoveries, and memories that only the two of them alone, yet together, would experience. Permit me to share some of the truths I've learned about this truly remarkable woman and how these truths will shine brilliantly, humorously, and warmly through the pages of this book.

Our adventure began the night we were introduced in 1979. I was a young, single preacher. My sister and her close friend decided to play matchmakers. They had just the girl for me, they announced. I was skeptical. They began their sales pitch by laying out the pictures of Joni's senior class on our kitchen table. I had to admit, the girl in those pictures was appealing, but pictures sometimes fudge the truth. (Who among us hasn't vainly imagined that we actually look like those retouched and airbrushed images!)

Joni was equally cautious. When, at my urging, my "dating service" invited her to join us at an upcoming church outing at an amusement park (remember, there were no "Dating Dot Coms," so I listened on the bedroom extension phone…with cord attached), Joni's first question was, "Does a preacher really like to have fun?" I've spent a lifetime convincing her—the answer is in the affirmative. They arranged a covert pre-date viewing and inspection that very Sunday night service where I was preaching.

Knowing she would be in attendance, I aimed to make a positive impression. I wore my best preaching suit—a peach-colored crushed velvet number (keep in mind, this was the seventies). In a feeble effort to up my odds of impressing Joni, I scheduled myself to sing that night as well. I don't know how effective the suit—or my singing—were, but I think the preaching had an impact. The following weekend Joni's whole family began attending our enormous 180-seat church. I also learned that night that, as pretty as she appeared in that senior picture, it didn't begin to do this Yugoslavian princess justice. I was smitten!

The hand of Providence intervened to get us started on our journey that very night. Joni locked her keys in her car, so I offered to drive her home. On the way I brazenly told her that I thought she was uniquely lovely (irresistible deep brown eyes of Serbian descent)—so beautiful, in fact, that I told her I would be inclined to ask her out if it weren't for my unwritten rule against dating girls who attended my church.

"So, where does that leave me?" she asked coyly. Thus, my first self-imposed moral dilemma!

We were young, and so was the church. Soon I found myself traveling the nation often with my mentor, Dr. Lester Sumrall, requiring me to be away from home frequently and forcing a courtship of seven long years—a period Dr. Sumrall would later teasingly refer to as "the tribulation period." It might have dragged on even longer had he not asked me point-blank, "Do you miss that pretty girl when you travel?" I said, "Yes, sir, I do!" "Then marry her and take her with you," was his stern suggestion.

Of the countless gems of wisdom I received from that history-making man of God, that was undoubtedly the finest. Joni Kae Askoff became my lovely bride on October 11, 1986. Two tributaries became one beautiful river of extraordinary life.

In the relentless flow of years since that day, our expedition has taken us through delightful, difficult, and diverse terrain. Hand in hand we've crested summits of unspeakable joy and trudged through valleys of profound darkness.

We were ecstatic when we welcomed Ashton Blaire to our family in May of 1989. She arrived on a Sunday morning to announce (rightly) to the world that she was more important than my schedule. (And this continues.) Two years later heaven blessed us again—we named him Austin Chandler. Our odyssey took an unexpected turn when, at the age of three, Austin was diagnosed with a form of autism spectrum disorder called Asperger's syndrome. This sobering news would impact our journey for years to come. Nevertheless, Joni's character has never wavered. Rising to the challenge, she threw herself into research and prayer in order to learn everything she could to help him progress—still priority number one for this exceptional woman. With love, compassion, patience, and cheer, Joni devoted her life to seeing Austin reach his fullest potential, and he has become that miracle in the light and warmth of her selfless devotion.

I was blessed to marry my best friend, who passionately believes her highest and noblest calling to be motherhood. I've watched with wonder as she transmitted her passion for learning to our children by giving them a love for reading and writing. Every school day of their lives they received a handwritten message from their mother on a napkin in their lunchboxes. Ashton still has a treasured archive of those napkins in a memory box, and more importantly, they are forever engraved upon her heart.

I'll never forget the day I found Joni washing dishes in our kitchen, weeping and gazing out the back window. "What's wrong?" I asked. Her response was profound: "God just showed me that washing these dishes and caring for my family was my purest form of worship to Him during this season of my life."

Travel a road with a companion long enough, and you'll see that person in the highest moments—the breakthroughs, the blessings—the times everything goes just as you had hoped and dreamed. Together Joni and I have certainly enjoyed our share of victory celebrations. But a road that runs for decades in this fallen, broken world will surely take you through some hard places as well. It is there, when life demands that you drink from a bitter pool, that you learn who you really are and the true identity and character of your traveling companion.

On my fortieth birthday we rejoiced at the news that Joni was pregnant with our third child. We were delighted. Suddenly, calm waters became treacherous rapids once more. Abigail went to be with the Lord before taking her first breath on this earth. With that loss, an unspeakable weight of grief threatened to crush the life and joy from my precious wife. When I fell apart, she simply pulled out her spiritual compass and found true north for both of us in God's unfailing grace. At a later moment she would write, "There is nothing in life, I feel, that changes the fabric of your existence quite like tragedy. While it may not define you, surviving tragedy will forever mark you. The wounds may heal, but the scars remain as a reminder of God's grace and strength that led you through 'the valley of the shadow of death.'"

Certainly we've had many more joys than sorrows through the years. Yet this is what I know: whenever a friend or acquaintance asks about Joni, my response is invariably, "She's just like God. She never changes."

Truly, she is the most steadfast of women. And what a traveling companion she has been.

As Joni will attest, one of my favorite movies is the miniseries *Lonesome Dove*. In one of the final scenes the main character, Gus McCrae, played by the wonderful Robert Duvall, is dying. At his side is his lifelong friend Woodrow Call. Together they'd seen adventures, battles, hardships, heartbreaks, victories, and loss. Gus's final words are: "It's been quite a party, ain't it?"

That's precisely what I think about this road I've walked with Joni. This unassuming country girl from Kirkersville, Ohio, possesses an amazing gift for communicating profound truth with economy and great wisdom with concision. In a few words she can deliver truths that would take me three weeks of sermons to accomplish. In her chest beats the heart of a servant. She is a tireless advocate for "the least of these." She's funny—no, she's hilarious! She is compassionate—no, she is the love of Christ "on display." She is deep—no, she has a depth of relationship with God few have plumbed.

I know you will love these snapshots of wit, wisdom, and wonder that are Joni Kae Parsley. "With grace in every step, heaven in her eye, and in every gesture—dignity and love." Enjoy the journey—I know I have.

—ROD PARSLEY

INTRODUCTION

THIS BOOK IS a reflection of my journey *and* my journal. Way too many years ago I was a college English major, and every class made me keep a journal as writing practice. I hated it then because someone was making me do it, but later I found solace in those blank pages and began to fill notebook after notebook. Occasionally I'd have an opportunity to share something I'd written, and when the Internet became a fixture, I decided to start a blog and share it all—the good, the bad, and the ugly! I've always wanted my writing to be honest, transparent, and relatable, and I really hope that it is.

Every one of us has a story. My story weaves an emotional tapestry layered with laughter, tears, questions, thoughts, errors, struggles, and experiences. I'm an *imperfect* person who happens to serve a *perfect* God, so this is not a high-brow, sanctimonious devotional filled with idealistic fare. This is also not a *how-to* book but rather a *come with me*. I am not a teacher talking to students, so there's no preachy discourse here!

Life is not easy, and my day finds me facing issues that all of us face; I write *about* it and I write *through* it. Some portions of daily life are mundane, some are stressful, some are joyful, some are painful, and some simply can't be explained. My prayer is that I can show that, regardless of any or all of it, trust takes the hand of faith and escorts us into the arms of a loving, sovereign God who holds our todays and our tomorrows. In other words, we are in good hands!

Our life lessons never end, and as disciples, we follow the Master Teacher. Jesus often taught in parables and employed a relevant metaphor to simplify deeper truths. In this collection of writings I endeavor to do the same by simply sharing my *real* life. I wear many hats, and some fit better than others! I have fumbled through changes, stumbled over difficulties, and tumbled down mountains I created myself. Through it all the gracious hand of God has kept me in ways I find simply amazing.

This is a peek into a journal where you'll discover everything from random thoughts to reflections, rants, and reality. I have a typical and not-so-typical life. I'm a pastor's wife married to a very busy husband with countless demands on his time. With that come many challenges for me and some pretty good material! I have a daughter who has left the nest, and the series of milestones leading up to that became a constant theme of a mom adapting to change and not really liking it! I also have a son, who at age three was diagnosed with a high-functioning form of autism called Asperger's syndrome. His story is interwoven with mine—just like his heart.

As you come on this journey with me, my hope is that you'll discover some common threads in your own tapestry, and especially this one continuous strand—the hope and confidence found in the simplest truth: *God loves you.* In those three words we really find the answer to everything, but often it takes awhile to get there, and I went many places along the way! So get ready, and to paraphrase actress Bette Davis, "Fasten your seatbelts, it's gonna be a bumpy ride"…but I think you'll like where it ends up!

The tissue of the Life to be
We weave with colors all our own,
And in the field of Destiny
We reap as we have sown.[1]

—JOHN GREENLEAF WHITTIER

Part 1

MIRRORED IMAGE—
PERSONAL GROWTH

W HY IS IT when we're young we can't wait to grow up? What's the attraction? When we finally grow up, all we want to do is recapture our youth. What's the attraction? We sigh and say, "Youth is wasted on the young." But is wisdom wasted with age? *Hmm...*

No matter how old we are, growing comes with growing pains. Life comes with those nights where we walk the floor and wonder why. There are those times that I ask all the wrong questions and know none of the right answers. However, I also know there is a remedy. A long, hard look in the mirror—not someone else's mirror either! Whom do we look like, act like, or talk like? These are the questions we need to be asking so we can get the answers we need to be hearing. I always say, "Growth is about gaining perspective, but Christian growth is about gaining God's perspective."

It's then that we can look into that mirror and not see our reflection anymore...just His.

> You, therefore, must be perfect [growing into complete maturity of godliness in mind and character, having reached the proper height of virtue and integrity], as your heavenly Father is perfect.
>
> —MATTHEW 5:48, AMP

LEAN ON

ALL OF US have had days where things are going along as expected...then something happens. There's an interruption in *our usual* that causes upset, to put it mildly. It's called *bad news*. It can shake us to our core, leaving us confused, bewildered, startled, and unable to breathe. We are left feeling helpless as we grope in the darkness of distress where we've been blindsided. We panic as we sound the alarm and cry out, "What am I going to do?"

If I'm being honest, that's my typical response. When I ask that question, I happen to be leaving someone out. I'm "leaning on my own understanding," which means I'm leaning on the wrong person...me! That scripture in Proverbs 3:5 begins: "Trust in the LORD with all your heart..." (NKJV). I'm assuming that means that if we trust God with *all* our hearts, then we won't need to lean on anything or anyone else. The passage continues to instruct us, "In all your ways acknowledge Him, and He shall direct your paths" (v. 6, NKJV). To acknowledge Him means to think on Him and about Him. In everything we do and face, we need to consider our Lord. In short, TRUST and BELIEVE!

If I think on Him, I think about who He is and has been in my life. I think of how He has delivered me out of "the lions' den" many times. On the other hand, if I try to figure out the *who, what, when, why,* and *how* of my bad news, I remember past failures, get confused and frantic, and start worrying.

There is another key component of trust and knowing that God has control found in Psalm 37:3. "Trust in the LORD and *do good*; dwell in the land and enjoy safe pasture" (emphasis added). What stands out is the admonition to "do good." Two words carry such weight! It causes me to do a little self-examination. Am I doing what I can to "do good"? Could this upset be any result of my wrongdoing where another is concerned? Do I need to change anything in any way? Above all, have I *considered* the Lord? It's obvious when we consider Him that we are focused on the precepts found in His Word, and it becomes the fabric of who we are. In other words, it becomes natural to "do good."

When we do that, we allow God to straighten out what we've made crooked! If we get out of our *own* way, He can have *His* way—and His way is always better! We can walk our path knowing He is the God who promises, "I will go before thee, and make the crooked places straight" (Isa. 45:2, KJV). God will remove anything that impedes our growth and victory in Him!

The apostle Paul wrote, "If God is for us, who can be against us?" (Rom. 8:31). Not just *who*, but *what* can be against the children of God? When we think about who He *really* is and has been to us, we can trust and do so easily. He has proven Himself to us time and time again…think of that! If we concentrate on our troubles, we become afraid. Fear strangles faith, but on the other hand, trust will be our companion on the path of safety when we go confidently in a God who goes before us.

Though it may seem like one to us, nothing is an emergency to God! We never walk alone, even though I must admit, sometimes the path seems like an uphill climb! *Sigh*…is there an end in sight? But, though I may wobble, I know to lean on the One who is with me. I tell myself to lean the *right* way on the *right* person.

I'm reminded of the powerful words of the classic hymn "Leaning on the Everlasting Arms," which speaks volumes, or rather, sings volumes.

> What a fellowship, what a joy divine,
> Leaning on the everlasting arms;
> What a blessedness, what a peace is mine,
> Leaning on the everlasting arms.
>
> Leaning, leaning,
> Safe and secure from all alarms;
> Leaning, leaning,
> Leaning on the everlasting arms.
>
> Oh, how sweet to walk in this pilgrim way,
> Leaning on the everlasting arms;
> Oh, how bright the path grows from day to day,
> Leaning on the everlasting arms.

What have I to dread, what have I to fear,
Leaning on the everlasting arms?
I have blessed peace with my Lord so near,
Leaning on the everlasting arms.[1]

This I know—God greets *our* bad news with *His* good news. I'll take that exchange any day! Just remember this, if you get tired while standing or weary with walking...just try leaning.

WWLD?

WELL, WELL, I got my feelings hurt. By hurt, I actually mean shredded! *Hmm*...what to do? Do I confront these people, let it go, or ask someone else to handle it? I asked, but I had no answer. Then the next morning, as the situation was still in the forefront of my mind, I heard it! I was bent over the sink, washing my face, and I heard these words: "What would love do?" I stood up, surprised and amazed! I never thought of it that way before. Quite frankly, these were not exactly the words I wanted to hear. I wanted God to say, "I will smite your enemies, and they are in big trouble for hurting you—they'll be sorry!" (Just being honest!) So I kept repeating that phrase over and over: "What would love do?"

I began to think of the love chapter: 1 Corinthians 13, in the Amplified translation. I've read it a multitude of times, but not with this perspective, so I read it again.

> Love endures long and is patient and kind; love never is envious nor boils over with jealousy, is not boastful or vainglorious, does not display itself haughtily. It is not conceited (arrogant and inflated with pride); it is not rude (unmannerly) and does not act unbecomingly. Love (God's love in us) does not insist on its own rights or its own way, for it is not self-seeking; it is not touchy or fretful or resentful; it takes no account of the evil done to it [it pays no attention to a suffered wrong]. It does not rejoice at injustice and unrighteousness, but rejoices when right and truth prevail. Love bears up under anything and everything that comes, is ever ready to believe the best of every person, its hopes are fadeless under all circumstances, and it endures everything [without weakening]. Love never fails [never fades out or becomes obsolete or comes to an end]. As for prophecy (the gift of interpreting the divine will and purpose), it will be fulfilled and pass away; as for tongues, they will be destroyed and cease; as for knowledge, it will pass away [it will lose its value and be superseded by truth].
>
> —1 CORINTHIANS 13:4–8, AMP

Of course, the passage "It takes no account of the evil done to it [it pays no attention to a suffered wrong]" stood out like a sore thumb! The NIV reads, "It keeps no record of wrongs." I knew what I had to do—forgive. There are times when we are to do the scriptural thing and go to our brother who has offended us (Matt. 18:15), and there are times when we are directed to do otherwise. For me, I was just given a simple question: "What would love do?"

I knew the answer. Love would do what Jesus, Love incarnate, would do. Love would do what 1 Corinthians 13 described. Love would do what Matthew 18 instructs. I knew I had to forgive, release these people, and not keep a record of their wrongdoing. But then I received a *new* instruction—to pray for them...what?! Pray for them...why?! Was forgiveness not enough?

Then I recalled the scripture, "Pray for those who spitefully use you" (Matt. 5:44, NKJV). I have done that in the past, but this time I understood it differently. Unconditional love wants nothing for itself. In other words, *it's not about me!* I needed to understand that these people had set a universal law in motion—you reap what you sow. They, and their gossip, had sown hurt and discord, among other things, and it was going to revisit them. Galatians 6:7–9 in the Amplified puts it oh so plainly!

> Do not be deceived and deluded and misled; God will not allow Himself to be sneered at (scorned, disdained, or mocked by mere pretensions or professions, or by His precepts being set aside.) [He inevitably deludes himself who attempts to delude God.] For whatever a man sows, that and that only is what he will reap. For he who sows to his own flesh (lower nature, sensuality) will from the flesh reap decay and ruin and destruction, but he who sows to the Spirit will from the Spirit reap eternal life. And let us not lose heart and grow weary and faint in acting nobly and doing right, for in due time and at the appointed season we shall reap, if we do not loosen and relax our courage and faint.

I needed to pray for God's mercy on their souls! I felt compelled, all of a sudden, because I do love these people. My heart was moved with compassion, and anger quickly vanished. Love was on the move! God's love in us can actually do this! First Corinthians

13 isn't unattainable! It's not just a pretty verse to read at weddings or to put on greeting cards. It is our banner—*Love is who we are and what we do*—because we are His likeness in the earth. It's by our love that they will know we are His disciples and thereby know Him. No wonder we are to, "Eagerly pursue and seek to acquire [this] love [make it your aim]" (1 Cor. 14:1, AMP). In this love are our completeness and wholeness in Christ. In this love is also our ministry to others. In this love is freedom to forgive and be forgiven. *In this love is our destination . . . every minute of every day.*

What would life look like, what would the world look like if we made love our aim? What would our day look like if we just asked the question and did so often: *What would love do?*

WHAT'S *in* YOUR NET?

YES, I WATCH TV. I remember the first time I heard our pastor, Dr. Lester Sumrall, refer to a television show, and I was shocked! I thought, "Wow, he watches TV like real people." Well, he rarely did, and I'm not sure someone didn't tell him about the show. Then again, he was Dr. Sumrall, and I am not. He was the most remarkable example of being totally sold out for the gospel of Jesus Christ. He used to say, "I spend thirty minutes a day on Lester Sumrall, and the rest belongs to Jesus." How many of us can honestly say that? Moreover, the question is, are we *really* true disciples? However, that's not just the question, but it's the challenge.

Discipleship is a word that has been tossed around so much that it's lost its true meaning. It's become such a part of our "Christianese" that it seems old and tired. But if we are to follow Jesus as we desire, then we have to follow the pattern given us in the Scriptures, which is specifically illustrated in the Gospels and the Book of Acts. Why? Because that's where we find the disciples whom Jesus called.

I have read and reread Mark 1:16–20:

> As Jesus walked beside the Sea of Galilee, he saw Simon and his brother Andrew casting a net into the lake, for they were fishermen. "Come, follow me," Jesus said, "and I will make you fishers of men." At once they left their nets and followed him. When he had gone a little farther, he saw James son of Zebedee and his brother John in a boat, preparing their nets. Without delay he called them, and they left their father Zebedee in the boat with the hired men and followed him.

Imagine what a presence Jesus must have had! These men had never seen Him, yet He called them and they didn't hesitate. They dropped their nets and followed Him. Not after a few days, few weeks, or few months; this scripture declares, "At once they left their nets and followed him." They left their careers, their families, and everything, and they did so *without delay*! Think of that! Next question—who among us could do that?

I'm a planner. I like schedules, lists, and predictability, which also means I hate surprises! If that would have been me, I could hear it now! I would whine to Jesus, "Now, let's wait a minute! Can I have a trip itinerary first? Where are we going? What should I wear? What should I pack? What will I be doing? Is it going to be hard? How long until we get there, and when are we going to eat? Jesus, You're asking me to drop everything? Seriously?!"

So, that brings me back to TV. There's a commercial for a credit card company that has the slogan "What's in your wallet?" When reading this Scripture passage, I was so astonished by the fact that these men dropped everything—and did it without delay. Without delay means immediately! As a result, I started asking myself a series of questions: "What's in *your* net? What is keeping you from dropping everything, every single day, to follow Him? What are you unwilling to leave behind, either consciously or subconsciously?"

Can we drop anything that's preventing our total surrender while also yielding to His direction as we follow Him? Can we drop past failures, guilty pleasures, or unforgiveness? Can we drop self-centeredness, willfulness, or an unbridled tongue? Can we drop a lack of discipline and just plain ol' sin? So...on and on goes the list of detractors that get caught in the net and therefore get us entangled in the affairs of life instead of following Him without delay. You cannot move if you're caught in something! I think *I* may be the thing in my net, to be honest!

The proof of desire is in pursuit. We cannot say we're disciples with lip service and nothing else to show for it. We pursue our passions, and who better to pursue than the One who called us in the first place? To pursue Jesus is to pursue what He loves...people. He didn't say, "Follow Me, and I'll make you fishers of power, position, and success while life is rainbows and butterflies"! He said, "I'll make you fishers of men."

In the meantime, we follow Him, and we follow *what* He is and *who* He is. We follow peace, we follow victory, we follow healing, we follow grace, and most importantly...we follow love. Yet while we are following, He is with us with that same presence that caused the disciples to drop everything at once.

He is the sunrise to every sunset, the heaven to every hell, and the tranquility to every tempest, and He is...without delay.

PETTY PARTY

IN THIS LINE of work, which I don't even like to call work, you hear people's problems. It goes with the territory and is one of the most rugged parts of the terrain. It's difficult to know when people are hurting and struggling, and often all you can do is pray and listen. On the other hand, there's the rocky road of listening to those who mountain-climb over molehills. It's in these moments that I dig deep and tell myself that my threshold of pain may be different from someone else's. There are times when people are really ridiculous, and there is no other way to describe their behavior but that it's *petty*. There, I said it! I have listened in utter disbelief, on occasion, and boy, do I really want to speak my mind and let my pastor's wife diplomacy go flying out the window! What I want to say is, "Have you ever known real heartache? Do you honestly waste precious time fretting and whining over something this silly? In the grand scheme of things, is this something that truly matters? In a world where there are wars, people dying, starving, and real suffering, does this register on the scale of importance?"

I know what you might be thinking! "Wow, how insensitive!" Well, let's see...when I spend time with a mother who is filled with despair as she watches her child suffer in the hospital, and then I have to listen to someone complain that they don't like the colors on the new sports uniforms, that's when I stare (or glare, rather) in disbelief. That's just one of hundreds of examples of what I've now come to call the *petty party*. Just like its friend the *pity party*, no one shows up but you and me. Oh, and someone else invites himself along too! The devil loves a party as he cheers us on and gives us more items to put on the *poor me* list. At the petty party we just get a different list—the "I am entitled" list.

We have been in a deluge of disillusion created mainly by the media that we allow to saturate our lives. This disillusion comes in many forms, but it all leads to the definitive conclusion that we are empowered to say what we want, when we want, to whomever we want, and that *me, myself, and I* have a right to do so. Guess what?

12

That may be the way the world sees it, but God sees it much differently. We are to "bear one another's burdens" (Gal. 6:2, NKJV), not *become* a burden through our words and actions. The Bible instructs us to bridle our tongues and be careful of speaking idle words. Even though these elementary truths are the ones we've known since Sunday school, we struggle the most to walk in them.

All of us, me included, have had a *petty party*, but it's time to grow up in God. As I said earlier, growth is about gaining perspective, and Christian growth is about gaining *God's* perspective. Can we ask ourselves, "What does God think of this situation? Is this something I should even bother with? Can my pettiness be replaced with His perspective on this matter? In the grand scheme of things, is this *that* important?"

If we could put someone else *on* the list and take our pettiness *off* the list, imagine how much we could accomplish for one another. Imagine how much freedom the Holy Spirit would have to speak into our lives since He wouldn't have to wade through all of our selfish clutter. Imagine if we could see as God sees and be mindful of what *and* who gets His attention.

So, the next time you feel tempted to have a petty party, just decide you're not going to RSVP! Instead think of someone you know who may be hurting. I promise they're out there, and I also promise that whatever petty thing is bugging you, it will pale in comparison to genuine hurt and suffering. "Confess your faults one to another, and pray one for another, that ye may be healed. The effectual fervent prayer of a righteous man availeth much" (James 5:16, KJV).

I guess it's time for a new list and a new party. I want my RSVP card always to read: *Joni Parsley plus One.*

GONE FISHIN'

AT CHURCH WE have a renewed focus on soul-winning. When I was saved in the seventies, it was during what was termed as *the Jesus movement*. The primary focus of that movement was winning the lost, and it was my first encounter with this novel idea called *witnessing*. We were hard core back then! As teenagers, my youth group and I went to the local mall and passed out gospel tracts and shared our faith. Somehow, in the current *me, myself, and I movement*, soul-winning has become a thing of the past and now pales in comparison to finding one's place in the comfort zone of faith.

We've never been called to be comfortable, only content! The defi-nition of the word *content* is quite interesting: "quietly satisfied and reasonably happy with the way things are; willing to accept a situ-ation or comply with a proposed course of action." *Hmm* ... I think I understand why the apostle Paul encouraged us to be content in whatever state we find ourselves!

We can find contentment when we are eagerly "about [our] Father's business" (Luke 2:49, KJV). If we read the Great Commission in Mark 16:15–16, it's quite clear why these were the last words of Jesus before His ascension. "Go into all the world and preach the good news to all creation. Whoever believes and is baptized will be saved, but whoever does not believe will be condemned."

Jesus was commanding us to do His work because He was leaving. He was showing mercy to the unbeliever because He knew their fate. He told us to GO! *He did not tell us to sit still in our church pews and drink coffee while we listened to a "please make me feel good" message.* If we seek the kingdom first, He'll take care of the rest, and we won't have time to think about ourselves.

Contentment and peace come from being connected to God. *If we love Him, we'll do what He loves.* If we love Him, we'll do what He told us to do. He knew that the secret of life, peace, and joy was wrapped up in our obedience to fulfill His plan—to establish

His kingdom in the earth. Only God the Father would have a plan where everyone involved would find LIFE!

As disciples, it's time to be fishers of men...AGAIN! We were lost and now we're found, so shouldn't we guide someone else to their future and their forever?! Someone helped us get there, so we need to return the favor!

RANDOM THOUGHTS

I F I WERE really giving you an honest look into my journal, there would be a random thought here and there. It may not be too "spiritual," but not everything has to be. So, I thought you might enjoy my take on everyday life—strange as it may be!

If you're an Ohio State Buckeye fan, you'll understand why I have a secret desire to dot the *I* in script *OHIO*.

If I could go to Africa with anyone and do missions work, I'd choose Bono.

Is it just me, or are men the biggest babies when they're sick...uh, no offense.

On the other hand, women can have malaria, pneumonia, broken bones, and be in the middle of childbirth and be expected to pack lunches, find keys, help with homework, nurse sick pets, fix meals, listen, give advice, break up fights, problem solve, plan the holidays, and execute all of the above and more with a smile.

My daughter calls me Joni at times—*hmm*...

My marriage has survived wedding plans, childbirth, the teen years, and remodeling...it's all a piece of cake from here, unless my husband retires.

I forgot, it has also survived all of my husband's illnesses (hence, the reason for men are the biggest babies comment)—he can be a bit melodramatic.

If I could meet any world leader, I'd choose Nelson Mandela—what a story...what a life.

I've always wanted to surf, but this requires either a wet suit or swimsuit, both of which make this wish not worth it.

When I was little, I wanted to be Miss America (whoa, dream big!)—my sisters and I used to play Pageant.

My dog, Balko, is snoring as I write this.

My favorite movie as a child was *Mary Poppins*—I got the doll when I got my tonsils out.

I can't believe that it's *not* politically correct to say, "Merry Christmas."

I can't believe that we have to be politically correct.

With that, I think I'll be saying, "Merry Christmas."

Why do I always have a bad hair day when I have to go somewhere, but it turns out great when I'm staying home—oh, cruel irony!

Seeing a blank computer screen, with a case of writer's block, sends me into a slight panic.

I always love people in the drive-through who stay at the window, pass out the food to everyone in the car, squirt the ketchup, fix the drinks, and then ask for more of something...I have need of patience.

The same goes for those in the drive-through at the bank who balance their checkbook, put their cash away, after they've counted it again, and then chat with the teller—I have need of more patience.

Honestly, I have need of just getting out of the car and not using the drive-through...when did we all get so lazy?

Balko is still snoring...rough day, or should I say, "ruff day"?! (Yeah, that was a bad one!)

Once I went to the grocery store at 5:00 a.m. in my pajamas, no makeup, and a ball cap—naturally I ran into several people whom I knew...oh, the horror!

Speaking of horror, when they were little, Ashton once painted her brother with water colors—I have the photos to prove it...always expressing herself.

She also expressed herself by wrestling a kid to the ground who pushed her brother and keeping him in a headlock...always the big sister.

Can anyone make it home with a hot pizza without eating a piece?

Can anyone make it to the McDonald's exit without eating a french fry?

If I could have a superpower, it would be time travel, although mind reading would be interesting, but maybe I don't need to know what people are thinking about me.

Drive-in movies need to make a big comeback.

How *did* I get my hair so big in the eighties? Answer—Aqua Net or Rave hairspray and a groovy perm.

Actually, you know you're old when your kids have Retro Day and it was when you were a teenager.

My son's laughter made me laugh 'til I cried tonight...love it.

When we told Ashton, at two years old, she couldn't say, "Shut up," she invented her own word anyway—"shugga." (That should've been a major clue of what was to come in the teen years.)

With that, however, her vacant room is still the saddest place in our house.

I love trivia games but get way too competitive...I don't know what happens to me.

I remember when nothing was open on Sundays except a gas station or two—it was called *Blue Sunday*...the Sabbath *really* was a day of rest.

I feel like my computer has a personality and is usually against me…I feel threatened by this.

When my husband drags me to the hunting store and tries on his gear, it's as if he's choosing a gown for the Oscars.

My kids have talked me into every pet imaginable, including the hamster I found swimming in the washing machine.

In the words of Aerosmith, "I don't want to miss a thing"…*really*, I don't.

No matter what train my thoughts are on or what stops they may make, there is something to make me smile and realize God goes with me and loves me in spite of it all. In the words of my domestic mentor, Martha Stewart, "It's a good thing!"

THE MONDAYS

I ALWAYS TRY TO write what I face in what is *real life*. Too often preachers act as though they never have an off day, much less a bad one. Today I'm having a case of the Mondays. For us, the weekend is often busy, but every now and then Mondays are just blah. I kept telling myself that Monday is a fresh start to a new week. I was putting on my Pollyanna face and even playing the glad game. What I wanted to play was the sweat pants and T-shirt game! I pushed myself all day and listened to that voice saying, "You can do it," instead of the one I wanted to hear saying, "But I don't feel like it." It's that same voice that says, "I don't want to exercise and eat a salad; I want the cookies." It's the same voice that says, "I don't feel like reading my Bible; I'll watch something mind-numbing on TV." It's the same voice that says, "Why be disciplined? I want to say and do what I want." What is this voice, and how do I get it to hush?!

Hear ye, hear ye...this is the voice of the will! It's the epic battle of human history—man's will versus God's will. Is your will David or Goliath? Can it be conquered? My battle of the wills is ongoing. It takes work every day to pull out the stones marked *my will* and hurl them at a Goliath-sized enemy called *SELF*. Self is, far too often, the god of our lives and the captain of our vessels. We often have the King Baby Syndrome—I want what I want, and I want it now! *Waaaahhh!* We don't want to wait on the Lord; we want our answers, our blessings, and our miracles through the drive-through window of a quick prayer, and, of course, we want to have it *our way! We don't want to deny the self; we want to exalt it.* After all, it's human nature, but...when we were born again, we were given a new nature—we were given *His* nature. *His nature also came with His voice. His voice also came with His will.* Hmm...could it be that easy?

Our nature, the nature of *self*, comes with *our* voice and *our* will—this is what Scripture refers to as "old things": "Therefore if any person is [ingrafted] in Christ (the Messiah) he is a new

20

creation (a new creature altogether); the old [previous moral and spiritual condition] has passed away. Behold the fresh *and* new has come!" (2 Cor. 5:17, AMP). It really is that simple. We need to stop wearing our old clothes! We have been given fresh, new garments! Why would we want an old shirt that smells like mothballs when we can have the one that has that Downy fresh scent!

We have to cultivate God's nature in us. I remember asking, "How do I accomplish this, Lord?" How do you become like someone? He gave me this analogy: an actor studies a person, spends time with that person, and works at developing his or her mannerisms and behaviors in order to capture that persona onstage. Likewise, we need to spend time with God to develop His likeness. And by the way, the world *really is our* stage.

John 3:30 declares, "He must increase, but I must decrease. [He must grow more prominent; I must grow less so.]" (AMP). If so, then His voice will get louder, and mine will grow quieter. Then His will can prevail over self-will. In the end, the winner is still us! *God works that way—always in our best interest because we are His interest.*

And so it's Monday. I didn't want to feel lazy, but what I needed was His rest—there's a difference. Time with Him is a vacation no matter where we are. It's a comfy chair in sweat pants if we close our eyes and believe. If we breathe in His distinction, He is our fresh air, our sunrise, our new beginning, and, if we will, He can even be our Mondays.

THE ELEPHANT *in the* ROOM

HAVE YOU EVER been around someone who knows your past mistakes? You know, the ones you never want others to discover. They are the secrets you keep buried in the deep recesses of your mind, but then it happens—somehow your past comes back to haunt you, and so do the feelings that come with it. They are those inescapable feelings of shame, guilt, and embarrassment, which then collectively lead to that awkward moment, thus the elephant in the room. You sigh, wince, get that pit in your stomach, and wonder who just poured cold water over you as your heart races furiously. The life begins to drain as you now wait *for the other shoe to fall*. After a self-conscious pause, there's the vain wishing that "This isn't happening," which then leads to the nagging question of who speaks first. Do you say anything or casually gloss over the obvious? Once again, there sits the elephant in the room.

We've all been there at one time or another, so there's no room for our sanctimonious attitudes! "Pride goes before the fall," as you may recall!

In a nutshell, here's how I feel about the past. We can benefit from our past in two ways:

1. Learning from it

2. Not repeating it

Other than that, what's the point? We can visit our past, but we don't have to dwell there. To visit our past can bring valuable reflection, but to dwell in it only results in guilt and shame. The Bible tells us that Satan is the "accuser of our brethren" (Rev. 12:10, NKJV). *He likes to keep us condemned by our past so we won't stay free from it.*

Now let's look at this from another angle. It's also not our job to bring up the past and use it as a weapon against someone else. We seem to enjoy being accusers as well...*hmm*, did I strike a nerve?! If we are forgiven, then our sins are under the blood of Jesus never to be remembered. If Jesus forgets, why can't we? How can we use the convenience of someone's mistakes to solidify our arguments? We make our case, in our own piety, as though we never made a mistake or misstep. You know the old saying, "Don't try to clean up somebody else's backyard until you clean up your own."

The Bible says it like this, in a very direct passage from The Message Bible:

> Don't pick on people, jump on their failures, criticize their faults—unless, of course, you want the same treatment. That critical spirit has a way of boomeranging. It's easy to see a smudge on your neighbor's face and be oblivious to the ugly sneer on your own. Do you have the nerve to say, "Let me wash your face for you," when your own face is distorted by contempt? It's this whole traveling road-show mentality all over again, playing a holier-than-thou part instead of just living your part. Wipe that ugly sneer off your own face, and you might be fit to offer a washcloth to your neighbor.
> —MATTHEW 7:1–5, THE MESSAGE

And that, ladies and gentlemen, is why I love The Message translation of the Bible! It may not sound pretty, but it's true! I love what author Jamie Buckingham once said: "The truth will set you free, but first it will make you miserable!"

The past not only needs to be history for someone else, but it also needs to be history for us. No inmate freed from prison seeks to be incarcerated again. The taste of freedom is sweet, and the only way we can go back is if we choose to. *There are always repeat offenders simply because they returned to the past instead of rejecting it.* John 8:36 encourages us with, "So if the Son sets you free, you will be free indeed." Freedom has no term limit or expiration date. Never forget that freedom belongs to us forever—and forever is a long, long time! This freedom flies on the wings of God's incomparable love and takes us, in the profound words of Buzz Lightyear, from the movie *Toy Story*, "to infinity and beyond!"

JUST KEEP PEDALING

H ERE'S A SURPRISE! I was whining to my wise friend
one day...shocker! I was telling her about a certain
situation and set of circumstances. I was complaining
that I'd been hoping things would change, doing everything I knew
to do, and was completely at a loss. My hope was fading, my frustration was mounting, and I was certain God had forgotten my
address. *Waah, waah, waah!* Her response to me was, "Just keep
pedaling." What?!

I was hoping for, "You poor thing; you try so hard. You're such
a good Christian, you are surely God's favorite. I just don't understand this! If I were God, I'd give you the moon and the stars!"
Where, might I ask, was the sympathy in "Just keep pedaling"? So
I requested that she please explain.

She went on to tell me a story. She was riding on the back of a
bicycle built for two. She kept asking questions like, "Where are
we going? Why are we going this direction? Aren't we going too
slow? When are we getting there, and how much longer is this
going to take?"

Finally the person in the front seat turned around and simply
replied, "Just keep pedaling." The moral of the story was that the
person in the front seat knew where he was going, how to get there,
and how long it was going to take, and he only needed one thing.
On a bicycle built for two, it's imperative that the riders are syn-
chronized as they pedal. If the backseat rider gets out-of-sync, then
the bike won't move properly. The whole idea of the tandem bike
is to find a cadence and work together to do so. The front rider
is called the *captain*, hence the reason he is in the front seat! All
that the captain needed from her was that she do her job...ped-
aling, following his lead, and staying on course. He didn't need her
questions because he had all the necessary information, so all she
needed to do was trust him and do her part.

Likewise, I needed to *just keep pedaling*. I was asking my
Captain all the same questions and growing impatient. Let's face it;

we live in a "hurry up and get it done yesterday" culture. Years ago I read a book that described us as no longer "Little House on the Prairie" but rather "Little House on the Freeway." We hate traffic, long lines, slow Internet, and delays of any kind. We have planners, iPads, iPhones, and other technology that keeps us as overscheduled as possible. *We don't have time to find a cadence with a leader, because we are too busy marching to the beat of our own drum and proud of it!*

We want what *we* want, when *we* want it, and that usually means NOW! However, it's vitally important to note that if we become entitled as spoiled "king babies," that same attitude will infect our spiritual lives and have disastrous results. In essence, we'll wreck the bike! To stay on course, move properly, and reach the place and answer that God has for us, we have to trust Him. Our answer may not come when we want it, and we may have to pedal uphill, but if we just keep going, we'll get there...*when* we get there!

If the answers came quickly, we wouldn't need faith. If we could do it ourselves, we wouldn't need trust. If we always knew the destination, we'd miss out on the trip and all the sights along the way.

Maybe I don't have all the answers, but I trust the One who does. So, in the meantime, I'll just keep pedaling even if it's uphill, downhill, or wherever. In conclusion, the immortal words of Walt Whitman keep reminding me that every journey has an eventual end...getting there is the hardest part.

> O Captain! my Captain! our fearful trip is done;
> The ship has weather'd every rack, the prize we sought is
>   won.[1]

MAGNETIC WORDS

ONE YEAR AUSTIN was in a therapy session with his amazing, gifted therapist. He goes to her to discuss his feelings and to learn to better express the frustrations and anxiety common with his challenges. I've tried to describe Austin, but a heart like his defies description. He is deep thinking and deep feeling, and he has a connection to God that I've rarely seen. In this particular session he and his therapist were working with magnetic poetry. These are just random words, on single square magnets, in a package. There must be hundreds of these little squares, and a popular thing to do is make sentences or poems on your refrigerator. In this exercise Austin was to use the squares to express his thoughts or feelings at that time. It's a great idea, and one would think that single words, here and there, would be what he'd choose. Instead Austin put this astounding poem together, and his therapist and I were absolutely floored! These words were so profound! It's as if an angel guided those squares...well, I think he *is* an angel, of course!

> Let every grace that's from above
> Create every gentle being
> Accept wisdom still new

Think of that! I have read those words over and over and over. They are God's words. We have to *allow* the grace of God—every bit of it. Grace is the unmerited favor of God—it's not deserved or based on performance; it is simply given. Then we have to let that grace create in us the gentle nature of God. Next we have to accept and embrace the truths of God's Word as relevant. The wisdom in those pages is ageless and timeless as though written yesterday. People argue whether doctrines are Old Testament, pre–New Testament, old covenant, new covenant, and so on. We don't get to pick and choose the parts we want or like. If that were true, I would choose the "Wives, submit yourselves to your husbands" (Col. 3:18) verse to tear out of my Bible! The wisdom of God is what Proverbs encourages us to seek, above all else, and is the pervasive theme of that entire book. Austin's words tell us to accept God's wisdom, often referred to as the "wisdom of old," as new again. What a message!

All God needed were some *magnets* to create *magnetic* words. What power we have with words, both to bless and to curse (James 3:10). Moreover, our words don't just have power; they have staying power—*they sink into a man's heart.* Proverbs 26:22 says that hurtful words "go down into the innermost parts of the body" (AMP). Words go there and stay there...they are magnetic. Another verse says that "the words of a man's mouth are deep waters" (Prov. 18:4, NAS). Haven't all of us drowned a few people then, if that's the case? On the other hand, our words can bless others, hence: "Let every grace that's from above / Create every gentle being." Our gracious words can create better for ourselves and others. We can become more like Him if we choose our words carefully.

Earlier on in Austin's treatment doctors and therapists told us to be very careful with our words. The wrong tone or word could cause a major upset or meltdown. Consequently we've always been so careful and guarded with what we said to or around Austin, and it was a great lesson to all of us. Because of that, Austin gets the best version of everyone, and the results are crystal clear. What would happen if we could be like that with everyone? What would happen if we bridled our tongues as James commands? There's a reason for it, and it's simple—*good words produce goodness.* Goodness is perpetual...it keeps going and going *if* we keep it going and going.

Out of all those hundreds of magnetic squares Austin chose to put together those words and that sequence. That message is for all of us. He said that those were his thoughts and wishes for people everywhere...it was his prayer, and it is our hope.

Hope is like the sun, which, as we journey towards it, casts the shadow of our burden behind us.[1]

—SAMUEL SMILES

Part 2

LIFE SUPPORT—ENCOURAGEMENT

I SN'T IT A good thing that we don't have to do anything alone? If we really think about it, we have a constant companion every second of every day. Like the old hymn says:

What a friend we have in Jesus,
All our sins and griefs to bear!
What a privilege to carry
Everything to God in prayer![2]

God never intended for us to be alone and go through the tough times without His help. He is with us in our darkest hour, and yet unfolds a beautiful sunrise just because we looked to Him in our time of need. He sees every tear and knows every hurt. He is a good Father, and we can run to Him and He really can *make it all better.*

He not only makes our paths straight...He makes them big enough for two.

Trust in the LORD with all your heart
    and lean not on your own understanding;
in all your ways acknowledge him,
    and he will make your paths straight.

—PROVERBS 3:5–6

29

EXTRAVAGANT LOVE

WHAT IF WE could begin to comprehend how much God loves us? Would our outlook on life be different? Would we treat another child of His with care, knowing how precious each child is in His sight? Could we let go of years of teachings that showcase God as this tyrannical meanie waiting to pounce on our every misstep or mistake? You know the one—He appears more like Godzilla than the God of John 3:16!

What has been modeled for us over the years in our pulpits, our pews, and our homes could lead many of us to wonder about this "God is love" message. Then, of course, mix in the ingredients of tragedy, heartache, and hardship with a dash of circumstance and stress, and you have a recipe for a *confused child of God*! If you didn't know by now, I am talking about myself and my journey from *How?* to *Wow!* It has taken me years to go from *How could God love me?* to *Wow, God loves me!*

Webster's defines the word *extravagant* as, "exceeding the limits of reason and necessity; extremely or unreasonably high in price."[1] One day I was sending a mushy card to my husband and best pal. I was thinking of him and how cool it was, after twenty-some years together, that I still loved being with him and that he was like my favorite slippers—simply comfortable. It was then that this notion of extravagant love hit me. It has nothing to do with material things that fade, but rather that which is everlasting. This love is why 1 Corinthians 13 says it is the greatest thing. *The Beatles were right*—all we need is love!

Think about that definition in terms of how extravagant God's love really is. This love exceeds the limits of reason because there really is no way we can wrap our carnal minds around a Father who would send His son to die for our sins. If that weren't enough, then He supplies our needs and does so beyond the limits of necessity, meaning this love is boundless. *It is no secret what God can do!*

Whenever we are feeling unworthy, think about the last portion of that definition, "extremely high in price." That's you and me! We were not just purchased with a price but with an *extremely high one*. God felt that we were worth the death of His Son. There is no higher price or greater love. And God felt that we were worth this love that only salvation can give—not just eternal love but extravagant love because...there is no greater God. And as for the tyrannical stuff, I don't believe it for a minute! I picture Him saying to me, "No need to be so formal. You don't have to call me God; you can call me Father."

HELLO, MY NAME IS...

W E WEAR MANY labels, plain and simple. Some of these labels have been placed on us by others, and there are some labels we place on ourselves. As a result, we get mixed messages that keep us from knowing who we really are and how God sees us. Our identities are often lost in what we do, how we perform, or what we look like. Think of growing up in school; we all wore labels—the smart kid, the nerd, the jock, the pretty one, the artsy one, the cheerleader, the trouble-maker, the mean girl, the party guy, and so on. When we graduated, that label disappeared into a future where no one knew us. But did it really? If we are constantly sent messages from others, they make a difference. We believe what others say about us and thus end up wearing the label that they apply. We venture into adulthood wearing labels that invariably say, "Hello, my name is...I'm Not Good Enough."

Labels have an adhesive substance so they stick, *but so do words!* That's why so much time is spent in Scripture talking about the creative force behind what we say. Words not only *create in our lives,* but they also *can create in the lives of others* as well. Basically we can hurt or help, build up or tear down another just with our words alone. I won't even go into what we can do with our actions— that's an entire chapter alone! Once the damage is done and that label is on, it takes a concerted effort to remove it.

How do we do that? I'm glad you asked!

First, we have to know the truth. We have to know *our* truth and *God's* truth. What do you say about you? You know your-self better than anyone, especially those who would say hurtful or negative things. If it's not true, then you can't believe it and cannot accept it...period!

Next, who does God say you are? You are His beloved! You are His dream come true! You began with a thought and were trans-formed into His likeness in the earth! You are so special that no one else has your fingerprints or your DNA—you are uniquely you. There is a place in God's heart that only you can fill, and you do so like no other. If you were an *only* child, Jesus still would have died for you. You have value, you have a purpose, and no person—or their words—can take that from you. You have the *real* truth, so accept it and BELIEVE IT!

Take every label that is negative or from your past, peel it off, and dispose of it! Now replace it with a label that says it all. This is the only label you need to wear, the only label you need to believe—"Hello, my name is…beloved child of God!"

GO TELL IT FROM *the* VALLEY

I REMEMBER BEING IN elementary school music class as we prepared for the annual Christmas concert. Since music has never been one of my strong suits, I wasn't too fond of music class. Our teacher was strict and expected no talking, which was like asking for my right kidney back then! He introduced this song for our class to perform called "Go Tell It on the Mountain." As we started singing, I recall how odd this song was to me. Since I had not yet developed the concept of abstract thought, or the obvious use of metaphors, I couldn't understand a few things. Why in the world would God want us to climb a mountain to tell everyone that Jesus was born? To me that seemed like a lot of trouble when we had phones, televisions, and newspapers. Then we had to sing, "...over the hills and everywhere"?[1] Was I supposed to be Julie Andrews twirling about and singing as she did in *The Sound of Music*? As usual, I drifted off in my own little world of imagination...I liked it there!

Even then I had this need to figure everything out—needing to know the reason for things. No one else seemed bothered by the words to this classic Christmas carol...they were singing away! I'd like to think my inquisitive nature was due to my undiscovered brilliance at such a young age, but I think I was just an odd kid! I mean, didn't everyone already know that Jesus was born? Did God need me on a mountaintop yelling to people? It was Christmas, for goodness sake, so it looked to me like everyone had heard by now. I'm sure my mind floated from that whole scenario to the Barbie dolls that I wanted or the Chrissy doll that had long hair sprouting from her head. (Only kids from the sixties and seventies will get this *and* that she had a sister named Velvet!)

Of course, I get the words and the meaning to this song now. The glorious birth of our Savior should be told, and it should be celebrated. Because of His birth we have the promise of heaven. We have that promise because of His death and, more importantly,

His resurrection. *The cross bought us our redemption, but the resurrection bought us our eternity.*

The cross has given us our undeniable life with Jesus, and we get it freely on a daily basis. *I have found that it is on the joyous mountaintops of victory where we acknowledge Him, but it is in the valley of pain and heartache where we find Him.* We find Him there, and we identify with His sufferings there. This is confirmed in Romans 8:17: "Now if we are children, then we are heirs—heirs of God and co-heirs with Christ, if indeed we share in his sufferings in order that we may also share in his glory."

It may not sound like it, but that is good news! Every valley points right to heaven, to our promise, our hope, and our eternity in glory with our Savior and King! Not every day is a valley, but don't we all have our moments? On the other hand, doesn't He also, in His tender mercy, give us "beauty instead of ashes" (Isa. 61:3)?

It's His birth that makes me want to shout from the mountains, yet it's His sufferings that make me want to shout from the valley too! He suffered and died, but He rose again! He didn't stop at birth or life, He completed it all with His death and resurrection…therein lies the promise!

Every promise became true and real and attainable with one phrase—"He has risen, just as he said" (Matt. 28:6), and *that* is something worth telling.

FIVE WORDS

O NE...day...at...a...time...We've heard it a million times as a cliché in a song or an overused piece of advice that carries little weight. But if we really think about it, it's an answer to the questions that we often ask: "How do I do this?" "How can I get through this?" "How can I get balance in my life?" "How do I get over this?" "How do I heal from this?"

What we rarely want is to be told that something is going to take time. We don't want a process; we want it NOW! We have developed into a Google society where everything we need is at the click of a button. *We have become so convenience-driven that patience and waiting are grueling disciplines that we'd rather ignore.* A process has a beginning, middle, and end—just like any good story. If we don't allow the entire process of healing to take place, we don't heal...it's that simple. If you skip around in a book, you miss vivid details and answers that allow the story to unfold as it's meant to.

When I was a kid playing with my friends on the school playground, we loved to hop on the teeter-totters. One of us would get on each end, and then one would stand in the middle. The object of our game was not to go up or down. We had to play "outside of the playground box," so our objective was to balance the teeter-totter perfectly. This took skill and adjustments on our part. We'd switch kids, or often put two in the middle, but whatever or however we'd adjust, we'd achieve our goal...perfect balance! I'm not sure why! I think kids are always creative on playgrounds...it's a good place for dreamers like me.

The reason I shared that story was to describe balance. *If we don't have balance, we go up and down, back and forth, and we end up in the wrong direction.* We grieve the past, stress over the future, and just try to get through the day. Dr. Lester Sumrall (our pastor and mentor) always gave us this piece of advice to avoid stress. He said, "I don't think about what I've done or what I have to do; I think about what is right before me in that day." I believe he was abiding by the instructions of Jesus in Matthew 6:34: "Therefore do not worry about tomorrow, for tomorrow will worry about itself. Each day has enough trouble of its own."

By saying this, I'm not advocating that we should not be proper planners for the future or learners from our past mistakes. This is about where we dwell. Do we dwell in the land of what *could* be or *should* be? Do we dwell in the land of what might've been or the land of what used to be? Or do we dwell in the land of what is our current reality?

By focusing on today, we make the most out of God's plan for it and can make adjustments along the way. We can also make the most out of our relationships. Today we can allow God to continue His plan and His story for our lives. *When you focus on the present, you can trust that God heals your past and holds your future. He stands in the middle as we teeter and totter through life, and He keeps us balanced.*

My wise friend had cancer, and she described how real those five words, one day at a time, became to her. Tomorrow was in question, and when facing death, her past didn't really matter. She would often tell me when I'd worry or fret about the future, "That's not for today." *Sigh.* She was right! Every day for her was one day closer to healing, not death. Her outlook was positive because she took, *really* took…one day at a time. She let God have His way and…*His* day.

SMILES

PRING ARRIVED TODAY. As I watch from my window, my favorite tree is getting dressed for its colorful debut. The rain took its orders and prepared the ground for what is soon to grow. The sun peeked behind the curtain of gray clouds to give us a sample of warmth as the breeze blew, and finally we could inhale the fresh air. It's been a long winter, and life has been hiding under the blankets of snow and ice. Life has survived, once again, and we can breathe.

Moreover, we are the ones who have survived. To be a victim is always to point the finger and to blame another. I prefer, regardless of the circumstances, the word *survivor*. I am a survivor. That word denotes strength, determination, fortitude, and good ol'-fashioned grit. We are not victims of anything; we are victorious because we made it! We made it through one valley after another, and, once again, we can breathe.

Survivors are stronger from the battle, but victims are weaker. Survivors depend on themselves and one other source...God. Victims look to everyone else for rescue and repair. Survivors are endowed, while victims are enabled and entitled.

I could easily say I am a victim. I've earned the right in several areas, but I refuse the crown and sash and will defer to the first runner-up to carry out those duties. Besides, *I'd rather have a purple heart than a tiara any day!*

A victim will say, "I want my life back. I want to be happy. I want a lifetime of happiness." A survivor says, "I have a life and happiness that comes in moments not lifetimes."

One of my favorite books is *Gift From the Sea* by Anne Morrow Lindbergh. It was written more than fifty years ago and is a beautiful reflection of a remarkable experience that offers stillness and peace to the reader. Every time I pick up this book, I begin to breathe. I feel the cadence to life begin to slow and my thoughts recline. This woman was a pioneer in aviation and a celebrated author, but she also tragically lost a son. The latter is what makes her a survivor. One of her well-known quotes states, "For happiness one needs security, but joy can spring like a flower even in the cliffs of despair."[1]

In other words, we can find moments that make us smile amidst the worst of days. We get depressed and frustrated when we wish for happiness as an everlasting state of being when the stars and all our conditions line up just the way we desire. We don't want to settle for happiness that comes in bits and pieces; we want our cake, and we want to eat it too! As a result, a lot of people are looking for happiness in all the wrong places and, I might add, in all the wrong people.

However, a survivor relies on joy because it brings strength. Happiness is a feeling. What makes me feel happy may not make you feel happy. Joy, on the other hand, always has a source, and we know who that source is. We *get* happy, but we *have* joy. That joy comes in knowing the One who brings the flowers in the cliffs of despair. We may still be on the cliff, but that flower is a reminder to breathe and know that He is with you.

In the last month or so I've had a lot to cry about, but I've had some things that made me smile too. Those are gentle reminders that God is still with me, blessing me and sending flowers in the cliffs as I climb in desperation. *He knows that if He rescues me too soon, I'll just be another victim of circumstance instead of a survivor of peril.* Nonetheless, His mercy reminds me of the words from an old Charlie Chaplin song called "Smile." It encourages me to smile regardless of what my heart may be doing, because life is still worthwhile no matter what…God made it so.

SCARLETT O'HARA

I'VE TOLD THIS story for years, but it bears repeating...even to myself! We had just moved into the house that we built more than twenty years ago. It was relatively empty because we couldn't afford furniture, but we planned to add as we could. Our kids were babies, and I was holding Austin, who was just two weeks old.

The ugliness of ministry had begun. Some things were said and done, and an ugly news story ran on the evening news. I was devastated. The report was false and portrayed us in a terrible light. I was holding my baby in an empty room with just a television set, and I began to cry. I was young and new at the persecution thing! I couldn't understand why these awful things were being said, and I couldn't believe God wasn't raining down judgment on all those involved in such a travesty of justice! Little did I know it was just the beginning, and such things would become a fixture of ministry life. When standing for morality and controversial social issues, one becomes a target.

Anyway, there I was holding my newborn in that empty room—I can still see it today. I walked around my nearly empty house crying and thinking. Finally I stood in my kitchen and made quite the dramatic speech. It mirrored the one made by Scarlett O'Hara in *Gone With the Wind* where she won't give up her land. I guess I was inspired! I even said, "As God is my witness, no matter what the devil does, he will never get my soul. I will never give up my salvation!"

I was sure that God and all of heaven must have been cheering! I could see angels giving each other high fives and exclaiming how awesome my heroic determination was! I thought maybe the apostle Paul wished I'd been around to write a Bible chapter about never giving up. Maybe Abraham was so impressed by my faith that he would tell all the other heroes of the faith about me. I was sure that in the face of this persecution my speech would have been seen as epic!

The next thing I heard was one of the few times I ever heard God actually call me by name. He said, "Joni, Joni...the devil doesn't care about your soul, nor does he want it; *he wants your effectiveness.*"

There you have it! No applause or praise for my speech. No promise that He'd smite my enemies. All I got was this! It was not comforting, but it was truth, and it was what I really needed to hear. When I thought of it later, I could see how merciful my Father was with His sweet advice.

The enemy of God will do whatever he can to distract us from our purpose, from our peace, and from our effectiveness in living the gospel as well as spreading it. He doesn't want us making a difference in other lives, so he'll first try to keep us from making proper changes in ourselves. If we can stay stagnant and stunted in our growth, we lose our effectiveness for God and His work.

We can never give up! We have to be *tenacious*, which is defined as, "determined or stubborn, tending to stick firmly to any decision, plan, or opinion without changing or doubting it; tightly held; persistent for a long time and difficult to change."

We *must* be resolute in our posture regardless of what is thrown our way! Maybe it's a little corny, but I'm not giving up any of my ground. In the movie Scarlett looked like a weary woman as she stood on her war-torn soil, shook her fist in the air, and made her famous speech. She didn't make her proclamation on the porch sipping tea as the beautiful Southern belle. She was fighting for something of value, something she loved, and she was tenacious and thus effective.

I learned a life lesson that day in my kitchen from a patient and loving Father and a lesson from one movie character...frankly, it was Scarlett.

MORE RANDOM THOUGHTS

ONCE AGAIN, IF I were writing in my journal, I'd be jotting down these random thoughts. This usually happens when my mind feels too fuzzy and tired to tie thoughts together to make sentences much less sense! So here we go again...

I wish my computer worked properly or I knew Bill Gates personally.

I wish chocolate was one of the four major food groups and had 0 calories and fat grams.

Instead I wish celery had the same fat grams as a Big Mac.

Why do we have to wait to get to heaven for our glorified bodies? I'd rather get it on earth since I will not care if I'm fat in heaven—I'll just be happy to be there.

Is there a reason most news anchors have bad hair? Is it part of the job requirement?

Wouldn't the world be a happier place if we wore our pajamas all day—who doesn't love flannel?

With that, why do we torture ourselves wearing shoes that are death traps?

Sometimes I wish I was Amish and enjoying the simple life...except I do need my hair dryer.

My son is right—I do look mean and scary without makeup, so the Amish thing really won't work after all.

Honestly, I wish life was more like *The Jetsons* (especially the conveyor belt that got them ready every day).

I wish reality shows had never been invented—I don't want to watch anyone eat a bug, date a less-than-perfect stranger, or be the next Mrs. 80s hairband vixen—what a sad commentary on society.

Could men think more like women and women more like men? Think about it...

Actually, could people just be more like dogs? Think even more about it...

I think Target was created by God...He saw that it was good.

I think my husband wishes Target was never created...I tell him God is in the aisles.

Since that rarely works, I tell him I minister there—it's my mission field.

OK, I have bought a lot of useless stuff there—how many containers does one family need?

Politicians annoy me...are they *really* public servants?

I leave notes on cars that park in handicapped parking places with no sticker—the fine should carry mandatory community service to help people who *do* need them.

Children may need to come with an instructional manual, but teenagers need to come with a muzzle.

I *still* need Bill Gates to fix my computer.

I love the smell of coffee but wish I liked the taste...I just want to go to Starbucks and order a Grande Mocha something with a shot of whatever and some steamed milk with whipped cream and sprinkles—just 'cause it sounds cool.

If I owned a business, I would want a children's bookstore like the one in the movie *You've Got Mail*.

The bigger the boy, the bigger the toy (garages everywhere are proof).

Cell phones—a blessing and a curse.

Texting…are some of the symbols Japanese?

Twittering, tweeting…what?

Does anyone still write letters? Getting a love text or tweet isn't very romantic, and you can't save it.

I embarrass my children…it's come to that…often I go out of my way to do so.

Husbands should have a label—*Some assembly required.*

You know you've reached middle-age when the first word you say when you get up is "Ouch."

People who need to "find themselves" don't know where to look.

I was a Girl Scout drop-out…I was in it just for the cookies.

Ahh, life, so interesting to observe. Not every thought has to be profound except some like the one that is ever-present—God is love.

By the way, I still need Bill Gates to fix my computer!

TWO-MINUTE WARNING

I was asked a question—so, how does one share the gospel in two minutes or less? The clock is ticking...I don't think I've ever said anything in two minutes! *Hmm*...my response is to first be the gospel alive and in living color. If Jesus could walk this earth encountering temptation and all things evil, and still remain the spotless Lamb of God, then we have no excuses. The apostle Paul said that, "Ye are our epistle, written in our hearts, known and read of all men" (2 Cor. 3:2, KJV).

A modern version says it a bit differently:

> You yourselves are all the endorsement we need. *Your very lives are a letter that anyone can read by just looking at you.* Christ himself wrote it—not with ink, but with God's living Spirit; not chiseled into stone, but carved into human lives—and *we* publish it.
> —2 CORINTHIANS 3:2–3, THE MESSAGE
> EMPHASIS ADDED

Um...wow! Obviously by this we know that people are watching us, and actions speak louder than words, but exemplary behavior says it all.

Beyond that I think *we* need to see what *people* need and appeal to that. Most people live in the moment, and eternity, and where they may spend it, is not always a motivator. Fear and judgment are certain turnoffs, as is self-righteous, condescending preaching. I think the best approach is always a caring one that speaks to basic human needs. We want to be loved, to be valued, to have a sense of belonging, and not to feel alone, lonely, or afraid. If we can speak to those needs by offering God as the answer and the alternative, then I think we have a better chance of success.

God loves us in a way that fills every void. His love is healing and brings comfort and peace. This love, as God's Word so beautifully promises, "make[s] all things new" (Rev. 21:5, KJV). With Christ, one has a new beginning, feeling loved and valued. He loved us so much that He died for us; that's how much worth He found in you and me. *Because of this love, we are His and find belonging in a place where we never have to face life alone again.* His love is a tangible presence that fills our hearts and tells us that He is with us...forever. The assurance of this love eradicates fear of the unknown because we realize that He holds the future as well as the present: "In him we live and move and have our being" (Acts 17:28). God keeps us...plain and simple.

When we share from our hearts, it's sincere and meaningful. We have a story and an experience; therefore we have common ground. All of us who call ourselves Christians had need of something or someone bigger than ourselves, or we wouldn't have reached beyond our human understanding and taken that step of faith to believe and receive. Because of that, we are witnesses of the saving grace of a precious Savior...*He paid the dearest price to call us priceless.* Tell your story and tell His story—for someone, two minutes or ten minutes can last them a lifetime.

THE PUDDLE *and the* QUICKSAND

T HE FUNNY THING about feelings is that they belong to us. They are personal and unique to our experiences. There are times when there is no possible way to articulate how we feel. Often feelings can't form sentences that make sense. I find myself unable to explain an experience that seems surreal, so I just stare in silence. I try to process my feelings, I try to make sense of it all and talk myself out of sadness, but should I? There is a time for tears, whether they roll down my cheeks or stay in the inner recesses of my heart. Some things are just simply sad. Some things are just simply hard. Why do we struggle to leave that place and the lessons that we can learn? Why do we want to leave the arms of God when He is ministering to us in all of His tender mercy? We want to rush back to vapid feelings of happiness because happy feels better—plain and simple. Sad feels sad and bad and, often, scary. We fear that the sadness won't end and will keep us captive in a perpetual rainstorm of emotions. I call times like these *the puddle*, meaning I don't mind stepping in it; I just don't want to get stuck!

In sadness we can still trust our Father. *He is our safety net when we walk the tightrope of uncertainty.* He doesn't promise happiness, but He does tell us that we can be content. I recall a particular time when our ministry was under attack, and we were as well. We were being persecuted in the worst way, and I was completely distraught. Our kids were just toddlers then, and I remember watching them playing and laughing, totally oblivious to what we were dealing with. I kept watching and enjoying their innocence when it occurred to me that they didn't have a care in the world—why should they? Anytime they needed a thing, we came running. If they cried in the middle of the night, we were there to comfort them. If they fell down, we rushed to them *to make it all better*. If they were tired, they climbed up on our laps and were gently rocked to sleep in our loving arms. They knew that their daddy and mommy would be there and take care of everything, so why worry? Their job was to have fun and enjoy life as little children should. It was such a lesson to me that day, and I've never forgotten it.

We weren't built to bear our own burdens; we were only told to bear the burdens of one another. The Bible tells us what we should do:

> Casting the whole of your care [all your anxieties, all your worries, all your concerns, once and for all] on Him, for He cares for you affectionately and cares about you watchfully.
> —1 PETER 5:7, AMP

In like manner, Psalm 55:22 says, "Cast your burden on the Lord [releasing the weight of it] and He will sustain you; He will never allow the [consistently] righteous to be moved (made to slip, fall, or fail)" (AMP).

Maybe I can't sort these feelings, and maybe I don't have to. My father has His arms open and ready to take it all, and then knowing Him as I do, He *will make it all better.*

But what else can we do when it doesn't end there? What happens when *life* happens? What do you do when every day feels like Monday? Better yet, when your world feels like a *midnight madness sale* and your credit card just got canceled…what to do, what to do?! You found the bargains of a lifetime, fought the crowd, fought a lady over a blouse, fought her husband over a parking place, arm-wrestled in the shoe department, waited in a mile-long line, and then, after finally getting to the counter, had your dreams dashed with a grouchy cashier announcing to the known universe that your credit card has been denied. You turn and commence the walk of shame, leaving your joy and dignity in the cart. Sound familiar?!

Life can sometimes feel that way. We depend on things and people and money, and all three can, well…fall short. Then we depend on circumstances to turn out *our way* and they don't…now what? We get handed the unexpected, the unpredictable, and the unwanted…what's next? This, ladies and gentlemen, is what I call *the quicksand!* It's living on *Gilligan's Island;* it started as a three-hour cruise, but after the storm you got deserted and are trying to make telephones out of coconuts with the professor and Mary Ann! Do you get my drift? (No pun intended!)

You don't get stuck in the quicksand; you just keep going

down, down, down until it suffocates you. Sounds graphic, right? I happen to think being overwhelmed and under emotional siege *can* take my breath; well, it tries anyway. It certainly has left me on the sidelines with the wind knocked out of me a time or two. Sometimes I just want to lie on the field or, better yet, just get carried off! There are those days when picking myself up, dusting off, and getting back in the game is nothing short of an Olympic feat. If medals were given for such gritty determination, I would be displaying my gold on the front of Wheaties boxes everywhere! Let's face it; we get back in the game for others…just the way it should be. If I didn't have children or people depending on me, I would've spent days on end shuffling around in my bathrobe and slippers in a daze, in front of the TV, watching *Judge Judy*!

Sheer willpower is an interesting thing. People climb Mt. Kilimanjaro by an act of sheer will. (And I'm not talking about laundry rooms or work piles on desks either!) Women go through childbirth with complete and utter determination. People will push their minds and bodies to extremes all for one reason—there is always a payoff. Be it medals, awards, accolades, championships, promotions, degrees, or money, there is always a motivation to get the payoff. For a woman in the throes of childbirth, the motivation is the birth of her baby. *The payoff is worth the pain.*

So what's the payoff for another manic Monday? Where's my motivation…I can't find it! "I've fallen and I can't get up!" I'm sinking, sinking, sinking, but ah, yes, I begin to hear words that unfurl like a banner of hope, "I lift my eyes to the hills—where does my help come from? My help comes from the LORD, the Maker of heaven and earth. He will not let your foot slip—he who watches over you will not slumber" (Ps. 121:1–3). *I may not be able to find my motivation, but I can always find Him!* I love verse 8, which says, "The LORD will watch over your coming and going both now and forevermore." He keeps track of our comings and goings; He knows every minute of every day, and He is keeping us all the while. With His protection and provision comes His peace…aha, the payoff! That payoff is like no other—the world didn't give it, and the world can't take it away. *Sigh*…I can breathe again.

BUT I DON'T FEEL LIKE IT!

YESTERDAY I HAD one of *those* mornings. If I had been one of the seven dwarfs, I would've been Grumpy! I had planned and organized the night before, but things still went wrong. I was chasing dogs in my pajamas, and they weren't listening—not to mention it was so cold! Then I was making Austin's breakfast and burned the french toast, spilled the syrup, worried we were going to be late, tried to get the dogs fed, and the car warmed up and loaded, which includes two of the dogs. I then remembered that I had washed my coat and scarf, and they were in the dryer. So I got the coat and the scarf, which were covered with white lint that I tried to brush but didn't have time, so I ran to get another coat...and now we *are* late! Whew! By this time I am frustrated but putting on a happy face for Austin as we drive to school.

After I dropped him off, I had a little time before an appointment, so I decided to wash my car. I go to the drive-through car wash, roll down my window to pay, and proceed into the wash bay. Oops! I forgot to roll up my window, so I am driving in with water spraying me! By now I'm not having a really good day! I realize that it's been a comedy of errors, and certainly nothing major, *but isn't it just like the enemy to steal our joy over "the little foxes that spoil the vines"* (Song of Sol. 2:15, NKJV)? However, as I sat in the car wash, dripping wet on one side, I said, "Lord, I really don't want to have a bad day." I continued trying to dry off, not expecting a reply, when I heard the Holy Spirit say, "Worship your way through it." "But Lord," I whined, "I don't feel like it." My choices were to worship or to stay grumpy. *Hmm*...what to do?

Now I realize there may be those who would question a Christian saying that they don't feel like worshipping our wonderful Lord. *The interesting thing about worship is that we have to take our eyes off of everything and everyone else, including ourselves, and focus our attention on God.* When we get entangled in the affairs of everyday life, worship can be difficult. It takes discipline to "throw off everything that hinders and...so easily entangles" us (Heb. 12:1), but when we do, freedom comes; moreover, peace comes. Here I was, knowing all this and having the answer, but still didn't feel like doing what God said to do. Why couldn't He just magically fix everything and not require a thing from me? (Am I the only person who's truly ever felt this way?!)

I remember Rod preaching on worship and how it confounds the enemy. *What does the enemy think when he tries to upset us and we fire back with worship?* We just told him that his plan doesn't work and he better think before trying it again! The most beautiful aspect of worship, however, is that it ushers in the presence of God and, "In [His] presence is fullness of joy" (Ps. 16:11, NKJV). When the cloud of His presence moves in, everything else simply evaporates. God's truths are so simple, and sometimes I am so stubborn!

Well, I *do* try to be an obedient daughter, knowing that He always has what I need, so I turned on some music. I had a forty-five minute drive ahead, so I had plenty of time to *worship my way through it.* I hummed a bit, mumbled for a while, and then a few of the words got to me! Soon the *unimportance* of that morning disappeared into the *importance* of my God and all that He does for me.

My day was not perfect and still presented challenges, but I stayed in an attitude of worship while being mindful of God and His word to me. As for the seven dwarfs, at least I can say that I went from being Grumpy to Happy!

HAVE SUITCASE, WILL TRAVEL

I HAVE ARRIVED AT a conclusion—I don't always enjoy traveling, but I do enjoy the destination. This all made sense during a trip to New Jersey. We flew to and from La Guardia in New York. Ah yes, one of the busiest airports in the world. My niece, Amy, and I arrived there to leave for home early on a Sunday morning, and we waited...and we waited...and we waited some more. Finally a young man made an announcement: "The flight has been delayed because we cannot find the crew." Yes, you heard me right—they couldn't find the crew! I didn't find this announcement comforting whatsoever. When people are going to get on an airplane and, let's face it, risk their lives somewhat in so doing, is this what you want to hear? Maybe he could've announced that the delay was due to a need to stock the beverage cart—I would've been cool with that. We were in a New York airport, so any delay would've been understandable *except* that the crew was lost! Well anyway, Amy and I had some laughs with that and the fact that our flight number began with 666. I felt like this was a plot for a bad horror flick called *Flight to Hell*. The missing crew, the flight number, and the preacher's wife were all good ingredients for your typical "slasher" movie.

Finally it was time to board, so off we went. We shuttled out to the plane after being packed like sardines in said shuttle. I was beside Joe Frat Guy—isn't there always one of those? He was talking on his cell phone for everyone to hear, "Dude, this party, dude, was so awesome, dude."

If glares could talk, mine would say, "Dude, are you serious?" I was reminded that I just spoke to a church about love, or I may have said, "Dude, you are also too old for the girly plaid shorts, and your visor is not very dude-worthy," but I refrained! I just wanted to get home.

As I climbed the stairs, I saw the next character in my movie, the frightening flight attendant. I mean no disrespect, but there was no "flying the friendly skies" with her. She looked like Phyllis Diller, seriously! She was not happy to be on the flight with the missing crew who, by the way, explained that they'd been sitting in the wrong plane...*whew*, I feel so much better now! If you can't find the right plane, how will you get me to Columbus? The plot thickens! We were finally in the air en route to Ohio...or were we? When Phyllis started yelling at passengers I wondered. This woman scared me; I'm not going to lie! Some poor people had the nerve to ask her what the snack choices were. I actually started telling Amy and people around me, "Save yourselves! The choices are Nabisco cookies, pretzels, or peanuts!" My heart was pounding as the cart rolled to our seats; I checked for fangs before I asked for a Diet Coke and then pondered, "How *did* she get her platinum-blonde hair that big?" Her hair was huge, as big as the sun, and as bright! OK, I'm getting a bit carried away, but you get the point. Eventually we did reach home without further incident, and I wanted to kiss the ground and cry, "I made it!"

So my travels have been amusing over the years, and I have the stories to prove it. Well, I can laugh now, but when I was stuck in a Rome hotel that looked like a maximum-security prison, I didn't find any humor. Or the time we were trapped on a runway in Sweden for six hours, and the plane's air-conditioning went out...not funny either! Now I can laugh and realize they were all part of the experiences that made up the movie called, *My Life Story*. In my movie there are so many interesting and colorful characters that have spun amazing tales. There have been thrillers, comedies, tear-jerkers, melodramas, and even a few horror stories, but they were all necessary elements to keep me on the edge of my seat. By the way, I hired my Executive Producer when I was thirteen years old, and we've been partners ever since. I met Him at an altar at church camp, and together we've created quite a story. Maybe, as I stated earlier, I've not always enjoyed the traveling, but I do know I'll enjoy my *final* destination and realize it was well worth the ride after all. I bought the ticket, so to speak, and I know how the story ends; it goes a little like this, "Eventually Joni did reach home, and she kissed the ground and cried, 'I made it!'"

Life is a trip, so pack light, pack necessities, and pack a sense of humor! Trips end, stories end, but there is an end without end that waits for the child of God.

NOTHING GOLD CAN STAY

Nature's first green is gold,
Her hardest hue to hold.
Her early leaf's a flower;
But only so an hour.
Then leaf subsides to leaf.
So Eden sank to grief,
So dawn goes down to day.
Nothing gold can stay.[1]

—ROBERT FROST

Part 3

REASONS for the SEASONS—CHANGE

WHO LIKES CHANGE? We might enjoy some change, but for the most part, we are creatures of habit and don't like our habitats disturbed! That's a BIG AMEN from me! Change equals challenge. With every gain there's a loss, and with every loss there's a gain has been my mantra over the last several years!

I love the Robert Frost poem because he uses the changing colors of the leaves to represent the continuing and inevitable seasons of life. What we can't avoid, we have to embrace. We can flow with each season that life brings and find the beauty in each one.

Regardless of what changes, God changes not. His unchanging hand can lead us gracefully from one season to the next and let us discover our peace and purpose while we're at it.

By the way, He is the "gold" that does stay.

> There is a time for everything, and a season for every activity under heaven.
>
> —ECCLESIASTES 3:1

WHAT ABOUT CHANGE?

I T SEEMS WHEN autumn approaches, we experience a great deal of change on many different levels. With September comes a change in season as the leaves begin their descent on the crisp autumn breeze while school bells ring and Friday night football games are in full swing. We have to transition from the freedom of summer into the rudiment of routine, all the while telling ourselves to settle into it. This is my life, and sometimes I feel that this is my life's calling—adapting to change! Just when I feel like I have begun to settle in comfortably, someone or something pulls the rug out from under me or the blanket from around me, thus exposing my uncertainty and anxiety relating to change. After all, we are creatures of habit. I like my same seat at church, my favorite chair at home, and I get completely freaked out when my local grocery store rearranges the aisles and I can't find my favorite foods. I like that which is familiar—who doesn't?

During the political seasons we're always overwhelmed with this overused word—*change* (on both sides I might add, so I stay fair and balanced). One party says change is good, while the other says their change was better—I'm always so confused! Change is change no matter how one packages it. Change asks something of us. Change asks us to trust. Change asks us to believe. And while this thing called change is doing the asking, it is also doing the telling. Change tells us to have faith, and change tells us to remember.

Ah, the winds of change! As a mom, those winds have tossed me to and fro on many occasions. From first breaths, to first steps, on to first days of school, then first dates, and first driving lessons. There are so many firsts and yet so many lasts. As our daughter packed for college on the last day she really lived with us, the winds of change that blew in felt like a hurricane! How could God ask this of me? I have loved this gift more than Webster could define, and now I have to let her leave as though she just rented a room for eighteen years? What was worse was that she was excited! I wanted her to be happy, but a tear or two would've been nice! Her dad and I looked like a couple of wounded puppies as we drove our packed car behind hers in what felt like a funeral procession.

When we arrived, we found elated kids and bewildered parents as all of us unpacked boxes and set up tiny dorm rooms. Our kids were taking their first looks as we were taking some of our last. As we said our good-byes and bitterly fought back the tears, we watched our girl go to her door and, yes, she did it; she twisted the knife—she turned around and waved with a face I shall never forget. WE COULD NOT SPEAK! And if you know my husband, you know this is a rarity! We drove in silence for a while, knowing that if one of us expressed an emotion the floodgates would crash open. This was change asking me as well as telling me. I didn't want to hear a thing; I just wanted to turn the car around and pick up my little girl. But change was telling me that I couldn't.

I had to do what change asked of me—to trust and to believe. I had to do what change was telling me—to have faith and to remember. It may be hard to do these things when it involves people or things that are never constant, but as Christians we have our heavenly Father who changes not—He is the same yesterday, today, and forever. He is the What, the When, the Why, the How, and above all, the Who.

One thing we cannot change is…*change*. As parents we are to give roots and wings and, eventually, work our way out of a job. We never retire; we just change job requirements…the title remains. God is a Father too, and He knows what it's like to watch a child leave to fulfill His purpose. *Every road we travel down, He has walked before us.*

Our answer and our reply to what change asks of us can be found in the comfort of our God, whose love is always constant and whose hand is gently guiding us through life's passages. Change tells us to remember so that when we're left staggering by those winds again, we won't forget the One who held our hand through it before. That hand holds our promise. That hand is as unchanging as His love, and that love, that kind of unchanging love…leaves me speechless.

And He changes the times and the seasons;
He removes kings and raises up kings;
He gives wisdom to the wise
And knowledge to those who have understanding.
He reveals deep and secret things;
He knows what is in the darkness,
And light dwells with Him.

—DANIEL 2:21–22, NKJV

A NEW NORMAL

WHEN THE FALL season comes upon us, a lot comes with it. I remember always hearing so many people discussing the recent changes they were facing, and every conversation was laced with angst and anxiety. I can't count the number of parents dealing with first-day-of-school jitters (not the kids, mind you, the parents) or a child leaving for college. I've talked to people changing jobs, losing jobs, moving, staying, transferring, downsizing, and the list goes on. People seem to be saying good-bye to life as it once was and hello to something entirely different. Yes, it's the dreaded word— eek, shudder, and even stutter...C-CH-HA-A-AN-GE!

As you well know, I'm not a fan. I am a creature of habit or habitat, whatever the case may be. I have my apple cart, and I don't like it upset. I've written a great deal about change, since it seems to be the ongoing theme of my life the past few years. I've adjusted my sails to these unsettling winds and have done so begrudgingly. When people tell me to "go with the flow" or "roll with the punches," I want to throw a few punches! They don't know whom they're talking to! I don't know the reasons why, but I've never liked surprises. I'm sure that Freud could tell me why I read the last chapter of a book first, have someone tell me the ending to a movie before I watch it, read a magazine from back to front, avoid any suspense novel or movie, and beg my family to never throw me a surprise party. Perhaps surprises, however good they may be, can be stressful or leave one feeling unprepared or taken off guard. I don't really have an answer, other than sameness and predictability equal a level of comfort.

Now that I'm done with my armchair psychoanalysis, I can move on! *Knowing how to walk in the moon bounce of change is something we all have to learn.* How do we move and keep our balance? It's like trying to live in a fun house where you look into the mirror but nothing is the same; it looks like you, but it's all distorted. There have been so many times I've looked at my life and said, "This *looks* like my life, but it doesn't *feel* like my life.

Something is different; I feel like I'm wearing someone else's clothes, and they don't fit."

I recently shared a conversation with a mom who was sending her daughter off to college. Since I've done that, I was the ultimate expert! I ended the conversation by reassuring her that she would find a *new normal*. Those wise words were given to me, along with, "You'll find a new equilibrium too." What, huh? A new what? I could understand the normal part, but equilibrium really threw me off...no pun intended! *Normal* is defined as, "conforming to a usual, standard, type, or custom." More importantly, normal also means healthy. *Equilibrium*, however, is defined as, "a mental state of calmness and composure; a state or situation in which opposing forces or factors balance each other out and stability is attained."

After a while I understood what she meant. When changes occur in our lives, our natural tendency is to focus on the vacancy instead of the ways to fill it. It doesn't mean we ignore the changes; we just find a new approach to dealing with them; hence, *the new normal*. When we determine to be determined to strike a healthy balance between *what was* and *what is*, then stability can be attained; hence, *the new equilibrium.* It sounds very *self-help*, but it's really a spiritual principle. Take a look into the notable passage of Ecclesiastes 3, which refers to everything having its time. "To everything there is a season, a time for every purpose under heaven" (v. 1, NKJV). As we continue to read, we find that each season has a cycle, which we cannot control or change. What can we do when left with this helpless conclusion? Acknowledge it, receive it, and believe that there is some benefit in this change, and then consider that God is the one constant moment in the momentous. I've clutched onto His unchanging hand through many changes that I've initially seen as disruptions. Later I've discovered the divine order in these times, and in so doing I have seen that steady hand guide me through and over some rough terrain.

Given the right attitude, change can be good and change can be God. It's up to us to be sensitive enough to know the difference. With every gain, there is a loss, and with every loss, there is a gain.

We can find purpose and growth in this new normal. We can find stability and safety in this new equilibrium. We can find *what* we need in finding *who* we need. I don't need Freud to do it; I just need a Father.

RANDOM THOUGHTS
on TURNING FIFTY

DEEP BREATH...gulp...yep, I am turning fifty. I have been pondering this milestone lately and have some thoughts. Actually, I wonder if I have so many random thoughts *because* I'm turning fifty. Are all my thoughts going to be random now? Is some cosmic shift about to happen because I've been on planet Earth a half-century? I have yet to do a huge life assessment or inventory of dreams, shattered or realized. I have been living this past year in blissful oblivion until a few weeks ago. All of a sudden, I kept getting questions and comments about being fifty.

There were the obvious jokes, the words describing impending doom, and the clever clichés. Don't get me wrong; I have a good sense of humor about it all. I'm not in bed with the covers over my fifty-year-old face as I rehearse my laundry list of regrets and failures over a tub of ice cream and a roll of cookie dough. Honestly, I've really tried to have a good attitude about it, but maybe I've tried a little too hard...so some of my thoughts from my fifty-year-old mind are listed here.

What am I supposed to think, when in one day I picked up my mail to find an AARP card, a reminder to get my eye exam, and an offer to purchase a cemetery plot? Did I just make some database for the elderly all of a sudden?

Will fifty qualify me for the early-bird special at Bob Evans and Cracker Barrel? Do I get the senior discount too?

Someone recently told me that I'd probably really like collagen injections or facial fillers...was that a hint?

On my driver's license I am listed as an organ donor. Will they tell me, "Thanks but no thanks, your organs are too old now; you can keep them"?

I've been told I'm fabulous and fifty, that fifty *is* the new forty, and that age is just a number. I've also been told that I can see heaven from fifty, and it's time to accept that death and one's mortality are more real than ever. That, ladies and gentlemen, is what I call glass half full...glass half empty.

I've been told that I'm officially over the hill. After I picked myself up off the floor from laughing at that one (I'm being sarcastic), I said, "Forget over the hill. I can't even get anything *up* the hill anymore."

I was asked, "When you look at your life, being married to Rod Parsley, what music can you hear playing?" My reply without hesitation was, "The theme from *Jaws.*"

Do I think that the best years are behind me? I can't answer that with a straight face because I can't really use *best* and *behind* in the same sentence at fifty...just being painfully honest. Gravity is a harsh fact of life.

My younger sister got me a card that said, "When you're fifty and it's harder to bend over to tie your shoes, you'll look around for other things to do while you're down there!" This is why I wear slip-ons.

If everything fifty is golden, then I assume that gold is valuable. If gold is valuable, why are there so many commercials to get your old gold jewelry sent away for cash? I suddenly feel very vulnerable.

I was also asked, "By turning fifty, do you feel like you have finally arrived in life?" I replied, "I'm not sure, but I think my flight took some detours, hit some major turbulence, circled for permission to land, got delayed a time or two, and got fogged in often. I did, however, use my seat cushion as a flotation device and kept my barf bag handy. It's been a wild ride, that's for sure."

The same person laughed and asked, "Have you *found* yourself though?" Not sure if I even know what that really means. Jesus found me, and that's all that matters.

Back to travel...that same Jesus took me above the storm and beyond the clouds. He was my constant travel guide and companion and will get me to my final destination...home.

It was my wise friend who told me, "You GET to be fifty! Not everyone *gets* to be fifty, to live fifty years, to love, to be loved, to breathe, to experience, to learn, to grow, to laugh, to cry, and to know God...all of it—good, bad, happy, and sad. You have lived! That is living!"

That being said, I don't need to do inventory after all...I wouldn't change a thing. Every experience counts as something earned or learned...even the ones we regret. For me, it's harder to drive a car in reverse; I prefer forward gear with my eyes on the road ahead. Rearview and side mirrors are only for keeping a *safe* perspective.

So, do I see turning fifty as glass half full or glass half empty? All I can say is this...I'm just happy to have a glass. *Mazel tov*!

AN EYE-DEFINING MOMENT

WHEN I WAS approaching the dreaded fiftieth birthday, I prepared myself. I tried to avoid those common, nagging questions, but to no avail. What have I accomplished in a half century? Am I really old now? Do I look old? Do I have regrets? Have some of my dreams died? What if?

Well, as I've said before, I didn't like some of these answers. I was tired of hearing the media propaganda that told me I was fifty and fabulous, age is just a number, fifty is the new forty, and you're as young as you feel. The truth was staring me in the face, from my fifty-year-old face, I might add! I was not feeling fabulous. I kept looking at the number fifty; after the year I'd had, I felt older, not younger! I decided to keep telling myself that I was happy to be alive for fifty years, and that I had been graced to come through some major life hardships and tragedy. I settled it, for the most part. Even when I got that AARP card in the mail along with an ad for my burial plot and pre-funeral arrangements, I was able to laugh and go on, trying to have a good attitude about it all.

What happens to us? Why is getting older something we dread? Someone asked me if I wished I was twenty-one again. Other than wishing I had my skin and weight at that age, I would never want to go back! I want to grow old graciously *and* gratefully. I don't want to pay attention to the hype; I want to pay attention to the gifts that come with age. I want to concentrate on the inside, not the outside. It was time to hold up the mirror...maybe the magnifying mirror that causes me to react in sheer horror! Yikes!

My fifty-second birthday was the other day. My husband and kids took me to lunch and then to the mall to pick out a birthday gift. Note to self: next time leave the guys at home. My son found the nearest couch and played games on his phone as my husband talked business on his. When we shop, my daughter and I have our own language, which guys would never get. It's our club, and boys are not allowed!

Ashton gleefully floated to the shoe department while I

meandered over to the makeup counter. When Austin was little, he said I had a mean face without makeup and it scared him…out of the mouth of babes! Anyway, I told the guy (yes, guy) working that I needed a brown eye pencil. He replied, "Good choice, black would be way too harsh for your age." A woman would never say such a thing to another woman! He handed me my eye pencil and added, "Have you tried our new eye shadow? It doesn't crease, which is great for mature eyes." What? Does that mean twenty years ago my eyes were immature? My mature eyes stared at him and the pink lipstick he was wearing in shock and dismay (and hey, I love everybody). The next thing I knew, he was showing me shades, and I found myself saying, "I'll take that one." I was sold…or was I taken? He was either rude or a genius preying on the elderly! I took my little bag of non-harsh eye pencil and crease-less, old-lady eye shadow and went back to the shoe department. Bewildered, I plopped on the couch beside my son and told my daughter what this guy said. She sat down, patted me, and said, "Mom, that guy doesn't know what he's talking about. Don't pay attention to him." I'm thinking, "Easy for you to say with your smooth skin and young eyes, but thanks for trying!"

What upset me was that all my self-talk had gone down the drain, like the hair color that covers my gray. I realized that someone noticing my age, and commenting on it, was as harsh as black eye pencil. I needed to settle some things and do a little soul searching.

What matters first is *who* matters. I was sitting beside my two children. I have been indescribably blessed to experience that kind of love—*a love that makes you breathe yet breathless at the same time*. Then, leaning against the wall, was my husband (still on the phone), and the gospel song came to mind, "Through it all, through it all, I've learned to trust in Jesus, I've learned to trust in God."[1] We've been through some stuff but faced it *and* faced it down together.

Of course, the list of people goes on and on, but topping that list is the One who found me so many years ago. He puts the *amazing* in amazing grace. The thought that I've been saved most of my life is a benefit that far surpasses creaseless eye shadow. God

doesn't say, "Well done, my young, good-looking and faithful servant." He cares that we serve Him by serving "the least of these."
I recalled what our pastor, Dr. Lester Sumrall, used to tell us: "I
spend thirty minutes a day on Lester Sumrall, and the rest belongs
to Jesus." Ouch! I was getting the message and the much-needed
perspective. Once again I settled it, and my discomfort dissipated.

My *mature* eyes have been privileged to see so much beauty and
so much life. They have shed tears, studied, watched, read, witnessed, been overcome and delighted...and counted fifty-two candles on a cake. Maybe I haven't discovered the fountain of youth,
and maybe I really don't need to. There is *another* fountain...I'll
take that one.

KICKING *and* SCREAMING

S YOU KNOW by now, I don't like change. I've noticed that that the older I get, the more resistant I am to the whole idea. Routines are safe and keep me in my comfort zone. Change takes me into the arena of challenge, and it does so with me kicking and screaming. I don't like unchartered waters and seemed to have lost my sense of adventure somewhere around the time I needed bifocals. My driver's license still has the same weight from my twenties, although I thought it would only be fair to add an extra five pounds after I had kids. I'm certain that the ladies at the DMV have quite a laugh every time I leave after renewing my license. It's only fair, to be quite honest, after having those hideous mug shots done, anyway, and they never let me have a retake. So I look like a serial killer on the FBI's most wanted list, but at least my weight is a number that makes me happy. If anyone ever questions it, I'll just say I'm bloated!

Part of aging is change in more ways than I ever imagined. Certainly weight changes and things shift and drop and settle like an old house. The scale is my mortal enemy of change, and if it could talk, it would say, "I wish you could see Joni on this—she grimaces, looks shocked and appalled, gets on and off several times, and throws me back in the closet as she screams, 'Why, God, why? Where are the Little Debbie snack cakes? Forget this nonsense!'" So sad but so true!

Things change, attitudes change, perspectives change, and reality most definitely changes. In my twenties I would work out in a coed gym and actually enjoy it while I looked cute in my exercise gear. Now I drag myself to a *ladies only* center wearing my old sweatpants and T-shirt, and even though I'm often one of the youngest women there, I'm still out of breath the entire way home. Again, so sad but so true!

Changes that happen on the outside are not as subtle as those that take place on the inside. I like those changes. I like the confidence that comes from experience. I like the assurance that troubling times won't last because I've been through some stuff. I like the growth that has resulted from pain and the perspective that keeps me looking for the silver lining in the clouds. I've been through the cloudy days, the rain, the thunder and lightning, and even a few hurricanes, and yet I know this…the sun will always shine again.

Change comes with years, and years come with change. Since we'll never escape it, we might as well learn to ride those winds of change. Some change feels like a gentle breeze, and some change feels like a tornado, but we can hang on to something unchanging nonetheless. "For I am the LORD, I do not change" (Mal. 3:6, NKJV). He is our anchor, our constant, our steady and invariable stability. *We can lean, we can fall down, and we can feel like we're drowning in a sea of change, but He is our next breath of forever.*

I may not like change, but I don't have to be afraid of it. I can see the silver lining if I look hard enough, and even if I have to put on my bifocals to do it, I can see the laughter behind the laugh lines. Yep, some change is not so bad after all.

PROS *and* CONS

THERE ARE PROS and cons to getting older, let's face it. Well, speaking of faces, that's one of the cons. Sometimes I look in the mirror and study my face like a science project as I ask myself, "What the heck happened, and who are *you* anyway?!"

As I reflect on my younger years, I marvel at how age has changed me. I am more serious but comfortable, much like my shoes. I think shoes are a major indicator of such change. I used to wear stilettos and didn't care that they'd cause bunions one day...my motto was, "Beauty is pain." Now I try on shoes for comfort, not looks—this came as a slightly sad realization.

As a young person I lived in the moment...in the carefree moment, I might add. I baked in the sun because deep tans were *in* and we didn't have spray tans or tanning beds back then. We did have this stuff called QT that turned your skin orange, and I mean *like a carrot* orange! Otherwise we got our tans the hard way, and it was like a part-time job for us! We would lie out on the roof, rub iodine and butter on our skin, and fry like eggs in the heat! Now that I'm older, I have hot flashes—I hate the heat! I travel with my own internal furnace, which came as a gift with middle age! I avoid the sun to prevent wrinkles and skin cancer, both of which were never mentioned in the 1970s. So I live with my pale skin, since I fear the spray tan ordeal—it appears way too complicated, and I don't fancy the idea of disrobing anywhere. As my husband says, "Some things are just beggin' to be covered up"! And...I must agree, which brings me to the next thing—dressing rooms. *Dum de-dum-dum!*

I used to take my young, skinny self and sashay into the dressing room without a thought. Now wild horses and a pushy salesgirl have to drag me in! First, the lighting is harsh and severe, as well as unforgiving...I need and want my sunglasses in there. I'm certain that the same lights that land airplanes are in dressing rooms. Next, what's the deal with the three-way fat mirrors? Honestly, I don't want to see myself at every angle. Certain body parts aren't where they used to be, and I don't need or want to observe this middle age milestone…and I certainly don't want to see it all showcased with glaring search lights! Then, you can always count on Miss Size 2 salesgirl to peek in and tell you how great you look. Seriously, do you need a sale so bad that you're willing to lie like a dog? If a person is standing there unable to zip a dress or looking like a stuffed sausage in an outfit, how great does she look? Besides, I can't see anyway, as I am blinded by the killer lights. I want to tell her to shut up and go eat some doughnuts, but instead I leave in utter disgust and despair as I look for the nearest chocolate anything.

As I walk down the mall, in my comfortable shoes, mind you, I swear off chocolate for the millionth time in a year. Again, losing weight was so easy when I was younger. When my tiny jeans would feel snug, I'd just not eat for a few days and drop five pounds. I liked working out, and I ate pretty much what I wanted. Well, those days are over! I have to eat lettuce leaves for a month before I can lose five pounds, and as for working out, blah! I sweat enough with the hot flashes, so why intentionally do something to sweat some more? I use the excuse that I fear dehydration…I don't know, whatever reason works at the moment. Exercise used to give me this feeling of exhilaration—uh, not anymore. I just feel old and achy afterwards.

Am I going to end up a curmudgeon?! I used to love going out on the town to dance the night away. I'd spend two hours getting ready and wouldn't leave until after 10:00 p.m. What?! At ten I've been in my PJs for hours, and bedtime is right around the corner! I'd rather have a good book by the fire and a few yummy lettuce leaves chased with a bottle of purified water…HA!

But seriously, there is an assurance that comes with aging, if you decide to embrace it. These seasons of our lives are inevitable, so why fret? There is a level of comfort and peace that comes when we determine to flow with every season God has for us. *If it comes from Him, there is always good to be found.* I don't look the same, but my outlook is not the same either. I like *me* on the inside much more now; I'm more settled and resolved and understand God on a deeper level.

I know what's important and valuable, and it's not in having a tan or wearing five-inch heels! Years are a gift—they add, not take away from our lives. With every year we are richer with experiences and the wealth of knowledge that accompanies them. I don't want a drink from the fountain of youth…I prefer the fountain of wisdom that has been packaged in the beautiful years God has blessed me with. Have they always been easy? No! Some days feel like a trip to the dressing room, but others feel like I'm up on the roof…carefree and loving life and doing it all in my comfortable shoes.

RANDOM THOUGHTS *on* WINTER

OHIO WINTERS ARE long; the days are short, the nights are cold, and the skies are a lovely shade of gray. Yes, I remember when we had a heat wave as temps climbed all the way into the forties! If you have endured a long, harsh winter, then you'll understand how crazy everyone gets when the sun peeks through the clouds that have been the typical dreary backdrop to our days and provides a bit of warmth to go along with it. It's still chilly, but it doesn't matter because we are going to usher in spring with sheer will, if nothing else! That said, I thought I'd jot down a few random thoughts on enduring winter.

To every person who lives in a warm climate and whines when he or she has to wear a jacket, I ask you to forgive me, but I want to smack you with my snow shovel.

To every person who shakes a finger at me for driving my 4-wheel drive Jeep while speeding by in a Prius or Smart car, I ask you to forgive me when you're in a snow bank and I'm not.

I'd drive a Prius if I lived in Florida, but in Ohio a skateboard makes as much sense.

That said—how smart is a Smart car? What makes it smart? Does it talk, read, do homework, pay bills, or recite the Bill of Rights? Just wondering…

What happens to us when it finally gets above freezing? I've seen people in shorts or no coats, grilling and sitting outdoors at picnic tables and driving their convertibles. I have concluded that we are *completely desperate* for some shred of summer!

By February we have had it! People are grouchy, bored, depressed, and ready to leap off of tall buildings! We have cabin fever, and we have it BAD! We are tired of coats, scarves, boots, and getting bundled up to brave the elements. We are pale and in serious need of sunlight.

When the sun does appear, we wear sunglasses and feel like vampires that fear the light.

Speaking of winter wear…I look terrible in winter hats. If I wear earmuffs, I look like an overgrown kid, and if I wear a scarf around my head, I look like Mrs. Doubtfire.

By February the charm of the beautiful snowfall wears thin. A cozy fire is now only a reminder that it's too cold to go anywhere and too dark to do anything. It looks like another night indoors in your sweats and slippers, eating Oreos and watching some weird show on hoarders or pawn shops.

The harsh reality of winter begins to toy with your mind. You begin to think you're really in the Arctic, and spring is never coming. You think you just saw Santa and the reindeer on the way home from work.

You begin to plot against that groundhog if he sees his shadow and we get six more weeks of winter. You look for the snow shovel once again.

I find myself identifying with the children of Israel in the wilderness…yes, I'm that melodramatic while singing, "Let My people GO!"

The happiest people in winter are kids when they hear the magical words SNOW DAY!

The rest of us are complaining way too much … sorry about that, Lord.

Speaking of childhood, why did I eat snow as a kid?

The color of winter is not just white. As I look out my window, and the snow has finally melted, everything is brown.

Am I complaining again? (Oops!)

Can I at least say that I am tired of even seeing my winter clothes? It's like they talk to me and say, "You again?!"

Even my dogs start to go outside on a cold night and turn around with this look as if to say, "Are you kidding me? What's up with this?"

Sledding is really half the fun if you think about it. Half is going downhill, which is fun, but the other half is going back up a steep hill, trudging through snow and dragging your sled behind you. Is it worth it? Yup!

Winter is seen as harsh and oppressive. It has its hardships but also its joys. One thing is certain—it's a season that's necessary. *We can't always see it, but life is happening…it's just hiding.* Spring is coming, and a new season brings its joys and challenges—both literally and figuratively. *Nothing changes if something doesn't change.* If I never see clouds and rain, then I can't see sunshine and flowers. In the words of the Disney classic *The Lion King*, it's the circle of life. Beyond that, it's also in the words of Louis Armstrong, "What a Wonderful World." In all honesty, I really have no complaints.

But if we must keep trusting God for something that hasn't happened yet, it teaches us to wait patiently and confidently.
—ROMANS 8:25, TLB

We must always think about things, and we must think about things as they are, not as they are said to be.[1]

—GEORGE BERNARD SHAW

Part 4

STATE *of* MIND—THOUGHTS *and* OPINIONS

D O YOU TAKE time to think...really think and not react? I can honestly answer that with two words: *yes* and *no*! Sometimes I really contemplate a subject, and other times I spew my opinion in haste. *Sigh*...another challenge!

Our thoughts take us places, just as traveling does. Along the way we take in the sights and sounds as we explore, endure, and enjoy one passage to the other. As we approach our final destination, we form an opinion based on our observations and make our decisions from there.

This journey is filled with enough unexpected trips, but if we follow our guide, we'll never get lost.

> "For my thoughts are not your thoughts, neither are your ways my ways," declares the LORD.
>
> —ISAIAH 55:8

IT'S NOT OK

THIS IS MY opinion, and just for the record, I'm preachin' to myself here too! So...if it's OK, let's take a look at what I think is *not* OK!

It's not OK to say what we think and feel anytime we want without any filter. I've often said if a thought could just go from the brain to a checkpoint before it hits the mouth, it would be great for all concerned! "The tongue also is a fire, a world of evil" (James 3:6). *Ouch!*

It's not OK for our words to tear down, subtract, and injure another—justified or otherwise! Words are meant to be healing, comforting, loving, instructional, and positive. They are to be strung together in the form of a sentence to edify and generate an affirmative outcome. "Out of the same mouth come praise and cursing. My brothers, this should not be" (v. 10). *Simply put, I guess that means that the mouth is meant only for blessing!*

It's not OK for us to vomit our nastiness and then say, "Well, I really didn't mean it." The Bible says, "For as he thinks in his heart, so is he" (Prov. 23:7, NKJV). In addition, "For out of the fullness (the overflow, the superabundance) of the heart the mouth speaks" (Matt. 12:34, AMP). *Um, there goes that excuse!*

It's not OK for us to showcase the flaw in another if we refuse to hold up the mirror and take a good, honest look at self. "He who is without sin among you, let him throw a stone at her first" (John 8:7, NKJV). "And why do you look at the speck in your brother's eye, but do not consider the plank in your own eye?" (Matt. 7:3, NKJV). Joni's translation—*Clean up your own backyard before you start looking in mine!*

It's not OK to use a tone along with our words that generates fear, belittlement, or ill-treatment. Hurtful, injurious words are a form of *abuse*. They damage and destroy when used in a thoughtless, careless manner, which is then passed off as a mere temper tantrum. WRONG! "Cease from anger, and forsake wrath; do not fret—it only causes harm" (Ps. 37:8, NKJV). Joni's translation again—*Before you know it, just a trickle can become a waterfall.*

It's not OK to use our words to judge. Again, so carelessly do we speak and think there are no consequences. "But I say to you that for every idle word men may speak, they will give account of it in the day of judgment. For by your words you will be justified, and by your words you will be condemned" (Matt. 12:36–37, NKJV). *Yikes, and again I say, yikes!*

It's not OK to use our words to murmur and gossip about others. Does tearing down someone else make us feel better about ourselves? Do we ever consider that we reap what we sow? Are we that imprudent? "A [self-confident] fool's mouth is his ruin, and his lips are a snare to himself. The words of a whisperer or talebearer are as dainty morsels; they go down into the innermost parts of the body" (Prov. 18:7–8, AMP). *It's hard to forget hurtful words…sadly, I remember many.*

I think I've *said* enough! I hope this is food for thought, because the Bible is filled with scriptures on taming the tongue and using our words to speak life and not death. There is enough negativity in the world, and as Christians we need to be using our words wisely. We are a light in a dark place, and the world needs our example, but first we have to stop hurting each other. Proverbs 16:24 (NKJV) says:

> Pleasant words are like a honeycomb, sweetness to the soul and health to the bones.

Our words can reflect the character of the One whom we claim to serve; He heals and loves and forgives. *His words to us are laced with tenderness and mercy because we are His beloved.* Just think of how He feels when we hurt someone He loves, and we use our words as the weapon to do so. It is possible to grieve the Holy Spirit, and we need to stop excusing ourselves while trying to justify our words or actions. It's not going to work, because there is never an excuse for SIN! I may be old-fashioned, old school, or whatever, but in my book, sin is still sin…and it's not OK.

LOST ART

I RECENTLY READ A study of how social media and the Internet are creating somewhat of a narcissistic society. The definition of *narcissism* is, "excessive self-centeredness and self-admiration; a disorder characterized by one's over-estimation of his or her own appearance and abilities and an excessive need for admiration. In psychoanalytic theory, emphasis is placed on vanity, self-absorption, egotism, self-importance, and selfishness."

The concept of this opinion was based on the idea that people spend time with a system that is singular. In other words, we don't surf the Internet in groups; we surf alone! *As we surf, the sharks circle the advertising waters and smell the blood—our wallets and our vulnerabilities.* We type and click, hoping for some fulfillment or satisfaction. Something on a website can do what people used to do, what God used to do, and what we used to do. Things that took effort and determination have been replaced with an app, a link, or a browser, so now we don't even have to leave the couch to watch a movie or go to church.

Life has become increasingly impersonal, and we are being blindly seduced. Facebook keeps us so *in touch* that we are *out of touch*. It may have its advantages, but social media keep us antisocial, if you ask me. We can ignore the kids while looking at a friend's life displayed on his or her little corner of the Facebook world. Honestly, it's not authentic. People only post the good stuff, and by doing so, as one psychologist recently stated, we have a whole new issue called "Facebook envy."[1] People see the lives of others in comparison to theirs, and it creates a feeling of inadequacy. It's hard to believe!

I appreciate technology and the convenience factor. I also see it as another vehicle that can be employed to reach people with the gospel, but... There are still many *buts*! Nothing can replace a church service with good preaching and worship that enraptures you. Nothing replaces conversations that are face-to-face... emphasis on the word *face*! I want to see a person's face—that person's eyes, smile, and expressions. People were made in the image of God, not computers, iPads, or cellular devices. Call me old, call me old-fashioned, but call me! Texting is out of complete control! I also want to hear a voice, hear the tone, hear the laughter or even the hurt, but I want to hear! I was driving today and saw kids playing ball, but one little girl who looked about six or seven had a cell phone and was texting and then talking! The interesting thing to note was that she was alone and off by herself while the other kids played. What are we doing? What kinds of messages are we sending to our kids, or do we, as adults, just send messages by text now and not by example?

I'm not being "holier than thou." I use a laptop, an iPad, and an iPhone, and I text, tweet, and blog. Maybe it's because I'm not very good at any of it, but I refuse to let devices replace people and things that matter by stealing my time and my attention. Websites can't fill voids, satisfy desires, or boost self-worth the way the gospel can. The gospel teaches us to follow the example of Jesus, who lived His life on earth for others and not for Himself. It's not our Internet server that completes us; it's our service to the Lord that satisfies. In that service we die daily to self and self-absorption by being absorbed by His presence and the needs of others. *Yes, we have to be self-caring, but not self-serving...there is a BIG difference.* We have to have boundaries and balance as well as moderation and modifications as we approach every day of everyday life.

Life isn't always about convenience; it's also about commitment. That said, I fear that we are raising a generation of self-involved kids with narcissistic overtones, unable to commit to much of anything. *We cannot enable entitlement.* If one is humble, that person never feels entitled. You can't stick your nose in the air if your head is bowed! We—as adults, as parents, and as Christians—have to work at providing examples of discipleship defined by devotion to a God who deserves our time; our blood, sweat, and tears; and, most importantly, our undying love.

So much has been lost, but one thing I never lose is hope. There *is* a remnant, there *is* a *Gideon's 300*, and there *is* still a church with *the* message. The eternal love of God is still the answer, and, believe it or not, there is still a needy world that is begging the question...it's just up to us to hear it.

PLATFORMS *and* SOAPBOXES

I SPENT SEVERAL MONTHS in contemplation and prayer before deciding to start a blog. I was unsure of putting myself and my experiences "out there" for people to criticize or evaluate. I felt like I needed to do it, nonetheless. I cast all fear aside and went for it! What a ride it's been! For the most part it's been an amazing experience meeting wonderful people and sharing thoughts about daily life as a Christian. However, I've had my fair share of negative comments—some hurtful, some ridiculous, and some that made me want to say, "Huh?" It's like my husband always says, "Opinions are like noses; everyone has one, and they come in all shapes and sizes!" To that I say, "Some noses need to be fixed, and that's why we have plastic surgeons!"

To be honest, someone told me once I should get my nose fixed. It has a bump from where I broke it as a teen and then turns downward much like my dad's. My nose is not perfect, but it has character and reflects my Yugoslavian heritage—I wouldn't look like me without my imperfect nose, and I'm OK with it. Just like noses, our opinions reflect our character and who we are as individuals. To be given a platform for expression was once seen as a privilege that people used with great pride. With that platform came the responsibility to use it wisely and circumspectly. Words were carefully crafted and treated as tools with great purpose and potential. *To have the freedom to express one's opinion was a trusted honor provided by those who died to give it to us, and, with that in mind, a reverence and humility underscored those words.*

Well, ladies and gentlemen…NOT ANYMORE! Nobody has to earn a platform; one is provided for you. With all the social media outlets available anyone can spew venom and do it with a haughty sense of entitlement. People can be snarky, critical, cruel, and invasive. They can spread gossip, invent lies, be sexually explicit, and use language that should make us blush…but we really don't blush anymore.

Social media have given us an amazing ability to access people. I think connecting is overstating the fact, but access may be, in my opinion, a better way of describing the benefit of social media. Studies are beginning to show how socially dysfunctional teenagers are becoming because they lack proper people skills and conflict resolution and management tools.[1] This is directly related to the lack of face-to-face communication, since most is done through texting, tweeting, and Facebooking.

It's amazing to me how brave people are behind a keyboard. Are we replacing our fearlessness with carelessness instead? As Ralph Waldo Emerson said, "People do not seem to realize that their opinion of the world is also a confession of character."[2] Do we care about character building ourselves—and not doing so by tearing down another? *Character building has nothing to do with anyone else if you really think about it…it's done in solitude, forged in decision making, discovered in complexity, and strengthened in adversity. Character becomes a noble attribute that defines us through our actions and inactions…our words or our silence.*

Having a distinguishable character is another God-given choice with God-given opportunities to match. We must choose and choose wisely. To be strong is different from just being strong-willed. Strong feelings and opinions don't necessarily reflect a strong character. We don't ALWAYS have a right to write or say what we feel. There is a reason for this scripture: "…a time to keep silence, and a time to speak" (Eccles. 3:7, NKJV).

There is enough negativity in this world. We should be the people drawing others to the gospel and the positivity of Christian life. I'm not saying everything is rainbows and unicorns; we also have a responsibility to expose the works of the enemy, but we can do so in an appropriate manner.

I guess I love the simplicity with which Richard Greenberg stated the following, "I appreciate people who are civil, whether they mean it or not. I think: Be civil. Do not cherish your opinion over my feelings. There's a vanity to candor that isn't really worth it. Be kind."[3]

Oh, how I wish I'd said that…

RANDOM THOUGHTS LIVE ON...

HERE WE GO again! More random thoughts that find me thinking and saying...*hmm*!

I spent way too much time trying to understand the difference in partly sunny and partly cloudy...huh?

I'm normally not impatient, but something happens when I drive; if the Rapture happens when I'm behind the wheel, I am in trouble.

What's the meaning of smartphones? Can only smart people use them? This has me worried...I have one.

I also have an iPad that was given to me as a gift. When will Apple come out with the iPerson who comes along with said purchase and teaches me how to use it?

No one liked my idea of the "antisocial" website called *Get out of my Facebook*—well, actually my daughter did.

Is it me, or are local political ads the worst commercials...and who comes up with them? Do actual people sit in a room and say, "Wow, this is awesome"?

Quite honestly, I wish athletes would stop going on *Dancing With the Stars*. I'm a football fan, and it ruins it when I see football legends in sequins and eye makeup doing the fox-trot.

WWJT?—What Would Jesus Tweet? I often wonder...perhaps, "FYI, Lazarus *did* come forth. #rosefromthedead."

If Jesus had a Facebook account, would He have a daily status update like, "Disciples and I just fed five thousand," or "At a wedding, just turned water into wine"?

Would His Facebook page have a profile like: Name: Son of Man?

I wonder if His photos would have titles like: "Recent Miracles," "Disciples and Me," "The Fishing Trip," or would His page have "Get the link to My latest parable"?

This may be why I had trouble with the idea of social networking, but if that's "the net" we need to use these days, so be it.

My husband went to the grocery store with me, and a) he messed up my usual route, b) it took an extra hour since he got stopped often, c) I kept losing him and wished I'd brought a leash, d) we bought twice as much and had lots of *man* food, e) he paid for the groceries of a sweet lady with five kids—guess it was OK that he went after all.

He also went with Austin and me to the bookstore—this was *not* OK; he kept chatting, following me, wanting a Starbucks, and commenting on stupid book titles and subjects (and there are many). Finally I suggested that he go join the other children for story time and that he was ruining my ZEN!

I told him if he wants to go to the bookstore with us again, then I am going hunting with him and sitting in the tree stand and talking the whole time.

His hunting truck is, well, indescribable. It's old, full of hunting gear, the brakes are bad, and my daughter calls it the "redneck hillbilly death trap."

Speaking of my daughter... she just had her college graduation photo taken—the camera flashed before my eyes, and so did the last twenty-one years.

She looked at me and said, "Mom, don't cry." On went her cap and gown, and, with a lump in my throat and tears filling my eyes, I decided she can never get married.

Wait... I changed my mind because I want grandchildren!

My son just gave me a random hug as I was typing this... enough said.

Random is an interesting word that means there's no pattern, connection, plan, or regularity. But random moments, thoughts, actions, and expressions make an *interesting life* out of an *interesting word. Often, we want long periods of sustained happiness and fulfillment, and yet bypass living in serene contentment through the everyday expressions of God's love and blessing.* Those expressions may be in a moment—in a hug, a grocery trip, a photo, a funny thought, or a thought-provoking phrase. When my kids did Connect the-Dots puzzles, they only saw the dots at first, but when they connected them they discovered what the picture was. Likewise, all our random moments do end up connecting the dots and, thereby, creating a picture...a life in His beautiful image.

SILENCE IS GOLDEN

I F YOU WATCH the news, there is tragedy upon tragedy and one story after another that leave us shaking our heads and asking, "How could this happen?" One such story was a shooting during a meet-and-greet with a US Congresswoman. This young man shot and killed six people and wounded many others. Some were severely wounded with bullets; others were wounded with the memory of it all and the horrific loss that occurred as a result. From such a senseless act families woke up, and their loved ones were missing. A mother and a father don't have their little nine-year-old girl. A husband doesn't have his wife; children don't have a mother or grandma, a father or grandpa...what can be said to that?

There is a time to speak and a time to be reverent. There is a time to choose words and actions carefully. There is such a thing as decorum, and there is such a thing as bowing one's head in silence. Some tragedies are unspeakable. There is no explanation for such horror other than there is evil that inhabits the willing hearts of men. I was speechless, and I'm glad. I just prayed.

Sadly, others felt it was a time to examine the motive of the killer and speculate. The rhetoric heated, and politics on both sides of the aisle became the debate. People capitalized on an opportunity to be controversial instead of compassionate. I'm not stating my opinion, because it's inappropriate. People are suffering, and the last thing they need is bloviating from politicians, news anchors, and bloggers. This is when we need our pastors and leaders preaching comfort and hope. People are scared and hurting. *When we feel threatened, we feel vulnerable.* We have a need for direction and certainty in times of loss and insecurity.

Where do we find it? My only answer comes from the lines of old hymns. I love old hymns because they are filled with doctrine and depth, beauty and poetry, unlike many of our vapid choruses of today. Resounding in the recesses of my mind I heard, "On

Christ, the solid Rock I stand, all other ground is sinking sand, all other ground is sinking sand."[1]

Then, I heard the awe-inspiring words, "Rock of Ages, cleft for me, let me hide myself in Thee."[2] I marvel that there is a hiding place in Jesus, a place hollowed out just for me...and so I go and I hide. It is there I feel safe regardless of what goes on around me because He is my security for now and for eternity. In Him there is no end...*In Him I have no end.*

When something is golden, it's idyllic, esteemed, elite, favored, a thing of promise. Silence is golden because it's that moment of promise and favor where we dwell in God's presence and listen, contemplate, or just sit there! In that moment we are special, favored, esteemed, and filled with promise because, in that moment, we realize that we are safe in His arms and we are His.

> We live within the shadow of the Almighty, sheltered by the God who is above all gods. This I declare, that he alone is my refuge, my place of safety; he is my God, and I am trusting him.
>
> —PSALM 91:1-2, TLB

In this place I don't have to talk; I just dwell in His presence, because He inhabits my hideout. I had hideouts when I was a kid. When we played tag, we'd run to our base or hideout, and we always yelled one word...*safe!*

TIME TRAVEL

I F I COULD have a superpower, I think I'd choose time travel to the past as long as I could take a cell phone, microwave, and blow-dryer. I think I could live without television, computers, iPods, and certain other modern conveniences. I could definitely live without the evils of the Internet and this oversaturated culture of twenty-four-hour news cycles where pundits sprout opinions like weeds in need of a good pesticide spray. When I grew up in the country, my sisters and I had to pull weeds along the fence rows, and we did it by hand! Weren't there child labor laws then?! Anyway, weeds were a nuisance, and so are opinions. When did everything get so out of balance? When did everyone become so entitled? Where is it written that one's opinion is right regardless of whom it hurts and what damage it causes? *Are we hiding behind freedom of speech and mistaking bravado for bravery?* Do we fool ourselves into thinking our opinions offer truth and information when, in actuality, that act comes at the expense of someone else?

At least the secular world goes after people shamelessly. There are gossip and rumor websites, tabloids, and paparazzi waiting for the latest indignity to highlight. On the other hand, believers are more insidious with their opinions and judgments wrapped in concern and condescension. I can take criticism when it's constructive and offered with a solution, but otherwise it's just plain mean. I've learned to ignore most of what is said because I know MY truth and HIS truth. I may sound morose, but I have had a *snoot-full* of the snooty! I am weary with being analyzed, overanalyzed, and under-analyzed by people—mostly by a certain group of so-called professionals or corporate elitists who wouldn't know the grit that gospel ministry demands if it bit them on the behind! Yes, I am on a rant! There is a method to my madness and a question I need answered. Why is it so difficult to reach people with the gospel? Why did it become this science that requires the dissecting skills of a neurosurgeon?

This is why I want to time travel. I want to go back to the old tent meetings where a preacher preached a sermon geared for the lost; souls were important because the preacher wanted to save them from hell *not* populate his church. There wouldn't be production meetings and budgets or marketing meetings to analyze the demographic and create ways to compete with modern culture...necessary or not. Back in my fantasyland, tents had lights that were strung from poles, not brought in on eighteen-wheelers with enough razzle-dazzle to make me wonder if I'm at a KISS rock concert (who, by the way, need to hang up the spandex and makeup). If the gospel is just a business, then I want to go out of business. I just want Jesus. I just want to see the lost come to know Him as I do. Why is that so hard to fathom?

I've heard all the arguments. In our overstimulated, overfed, overscheduled, and overwhelmed culture we have to be relevant to compete with what's available to Joe Q. Public and his wife and kids. I agree and I understand, but have we gone overboard in our attempts and now just look silly and cartoonish? I think relevance is more than wearing torn jeans and a leather choker so a preacher can seem hip and cool. I do know this: cool people don't have to try to be cool; they just are. I also know this: preachers who have something to say and God's anointing to say it don't need to be *cutting-edge. Fads die; truth does not!*

People should have status because they have substance. The proof of substance is always found in one's work, and as a result, that work is a lasting legacy. I never see the classic books by the great authors on the clearance table at the bookstore. Their work is legendary: Jane Austen's *Pride and Prejudice*, John Steinbeck's *Of Mice and Men*, Harper Lee's *To Kill a Mockingbird*, J. D. Salinger's *Catcher in the Rye*, Emily Bronte's *Wuthering Heights*, Homer's *Odyssey*, Dante's *The Divine Comedy*, and C. S. Lewis's *Mere Christianity*. These were among a few classics that I read more than twenty-five years ago, but they are still sold today...at full price, I might add. That's why their work is always referred to as *enduring. Do we want enduring or relevant?* Do we want true conversions at an altar, or are we satisfied with our bulging mailing lists, overindulged congregations, and underwhelming Christian experience? Is being so friendly, so fuzzy, and so fussy working? Is all this to-do effecting the change we really want…is this it?

When was serving God with one's whole heart and soul ever meant to be convenient? Freedom comes with a price, not a cup of coffee and a buffet of services that fit one's taste and schedule. If people want to live for God and be in any ministry, get ready for a four-letter word…PAIN! Nobody wants to discuss that…what a downer! We don't teach people how to persevere anymore, and that's why they quit and divorce the church. We highlight the honeymoon, not the sleepless nights with the screaming baby. *The world does not need more of the world!* We don't have to dress like teenagers to reach them. God is *better* than that; His gospel message of redemption *deserves better* than that, and I still believe there are people who want *more* than that.

I am bewildered because I listen, I read, I try to stay current, and it's all gobbledygook to me. I confess, for whatever reason, I just don't get it, and I am not sure I want to. I guess the subject of *engaging the culture* is too broad, and I just wish we could engage our neighbor, family member, and coworker first. *Maybe the problem is the lack of Christ-likeness in our Christianity* (and I didn't need a marketing degree to figure that one out). I really don't mind that I get treated like the country bumpkin that I am, because I'm country enough to say, "Get off your high horse long enough to see the manure you're leaving behind when you think it's fine to offend God by diluting His message as long as we don't offend anybody else." Argue all you want, but try your one-sided argument from my side of the table just once. Stop being so cliché, and please, for the love of the Almighty, stop imitating TV characters from *Mad Men* and *The Apprentice* long enough to FEEL. Stop seeing the nobility in your work long enough to take a look at a wrecked life in need of rescue and be a hero. Whew! That ends my "Jesus turning the tables over in the temple" rant! I've heard many explanations for Jesus and His angry display in that passage, but I think it was simply that *the Son* saw people who were offending *the Father.*

What we don't understand, we like to ignore. This is why I want to engage my superpowers to time-travel back to a simpler time where one could echo the declaration of the apostle Paul: "Follow me as I follow Christ." (See 1 Corinthians 11:1.) The difference is, Paul *really* did follow Christ, and it cost him everything...even his life. That message is not quite marketable by today's standards, but in my fantasy it would be met with eager applause and total abandonment to the cause of Jesus, the true and living Savior.

Sigh...perhaps the professionals are right with all their highbrow analysis; this idealist just wishes it wasn't so. Maybe I *get it* after all; I just don't want to *have* to get it. It is, however, possible to hold two contrasting realities at the same time. Charles Dickens said it in *A Tale of Two Cities*: "It was the best of times, it was the worst of times."

RANDOM THOUGHTS
FROM VACATION

SINCE MY HUSBAND was on this Apex Summer Bus tour, we decided to tag along for part of it, then rent the bus for a few days' vacation. Austin thought the tour bus was really cool and wanted to take a road trip. As a result, I had a lot of time to think, and since my thoughts are so random, as we know, I thought I'd share some of them, so here we go…again!

A week with my kids and life runs a reverse, like in football; when did I start getting treated like the kid?

The phrase "Kids should be seen and not heard" seems to have been rephrased—"Parents should be seen and not heard unless they are handing out the Visa card."

Travels on a tour bus—way too close, way too long, and way too much listening to my husband talk on the cell phone and talk… talk…talk…and talk some more.

Since I'm treated like a ten-year-old, I decide to act like one. I start repeating everything he says during his phone conversation. I think I'm funny…he apparently does not.

After a while I am irritated; he won't hush…feeling a bit crazy by now. Perhaps I'll smother him with a pillow.

The freeway is not a scenic drive…I am bored and everyone is asleep. What to do? I may dismantle the cell phone.

Reflecting on our last few days, I came to this conclusion: fanny packs are alive and well and on fannies everywhere!

Another conclusion—my husband never stops working. Thanks to cell phones and conference calls, he continued to get the following as I kept walking by: the evil eye, the huge sigh, the shaking of the head, the "I'm gonna smother you with a pillow" face, the tapping on the watch, the tapping of the foot, the rolling of the eyes, the flaring of the nostrils (he hates that!), so more flaring of the nostrils, more sighing, and nothing works...I plot my revenge.

He's still talking...I'm still plotting. We're staying in a mountain cabin where there are bears...the possibilities are endless.

Maybe I'll buy a fanny pack; not exactly an area I wish to highlight, but they do seem rather handy and practical.

I doze off on the bus to wake suddenly disoriented: "Am I in hell? Was it the plot to smother husband with the pillow that got me here? I was kidding, really!"

I make a decision: separate vacations next year! Husband and cell phone can go on a couples cruise.

The kids paid their dues, did the old folks a favor, and are officially off the hook. They can go wherever they can afford...the backyard is lovely this time of year, by the way.

My Visa and I will be heading off together sans Chatty Cathy, sans the bus, and sans the kids who kept looking at each other sending telepathic messages like, "Can you believe these two?"

I dream of being Anne Morrow Lindbergh in complete solitude on a beach, writing her classic *Gift From the Sea*. Instead, as I travel down the freeway, my life feels more like a bad country song.

Since I'm in Tennessee, I feel inspired!

Dreams may fade like kitchen curtains,
But what I know is *God is certain*.
Maybe I'm not always steady,
But my fanny pack and I are ready!

Sometimes I think I tried too hard to recapture the magic of a day and time that has passed; time to realize it and make some necessary adjustments so this season of life fits, and then I can enjoy wearing it.

By the way, where would I find a fanny pack? Is there a fanny pack store? A fanny pack website? A fanny pack department at Walmart? Get back to me on that!

We spend precious hours fearing the inevitable. It would be wise to use that time adoring our families, cherishing our friends and living our lives.[1]

—MAYA ANGELOU

Part 5

COLORFUL CHARACTERS—FAMILY, MOTHERHOOD, RELATIONSHIPS

L IKE IT OR not, is there anything more important than people? Other than our own salvation, most of the gospel message concerns our service to others. Oh, boy, another challenge…life is filled with people!

Our stories have a cast of characters who play all types of roles: heroes, villains, stars, supporting players, and extras. Every role is important to the story and to the lesson we learn from it.

God is the author and finisher of our faith—our story has a beginning and an ending. So when we laugh, cry, think, and learn, we can find all the elements of a good movie…but He gets the writing credits!

> If you really keep the royal law found in Scripture, "'Love your neighbor as yourself," you are doing right.
>
> —JAMES 2:8

MY YEARS *as a* MOM

ONE DAY I was invited to speak at our mom's group at our church. I thought of those years beginning as a new mom, and then I compared them to my thoughts and feelings twenty-some years later.

There are so many things I've learned as a mom; the pay may not be much, but the reward is indescribable. The moment I laid my eyes on my babies, I felt a love that said, "I'll die for you, and I'll live for you." What a gift, what an honor...how was I worthy? With that mind-set I set out to prove that I was and to tell God that He could trust me with these eternal beings. *I marveled as I watched them sleep, laughed at every cute thing they did, and wondered how, with one smile, my heart could melt and be captured all at once.*

Being a mom is just plain ol' hard work and a balancing act of Cirque de Soleil proportions! But, at the end of the day, when I'd plowed through a mountain of laundry, cleaned spilled juice, wiped noses, picked up the trail of toys, found Cheerios in the oddest of places, and collapsed into bed, only to have one or both crawl in with me at some point, I was still thankful beyond measure. *I was tired but never too tired.* I had my job description and was determined to fulfill it; I knew I'd never get a raise, but every day they were my bonus and my paid vacation. To see the world through their eyes, and to feel it through their innocent hearts, was God's way of skywriting the recipe for pure delight.

The years flew by too quickly as I went from packing diaper bags to packing lunches and backpacks and then, packing away childhood when one readied for the end of high school and the other left for college. In those boxes were years of treasured wonderment, and as I secured each lid, I fastened a piece of my heart with them. *The seasons of life are undeniable...they come, they go, they don't last long enough, or, in the case of the teen years, they last too long!* Nonetheless, with each season there was a tireless investment and a sincere hope that I embraced every second and realized how precious it was. My years as a mom of toddlers are long gone, my years as a mom of school-agers are gone, and my years with teenagers are gone (no regret there!). I will never buy school uniforms or school supplies again. I was there when they took their first steps, and I've been there with every milestone too. My house no longer reverberates with the sounds of teenage girls giggling over their latest crush, practicing cheers, or listening to their favorite boy band. My kitchen counter isn't covered with the latest class project or homework needing to be done. I now watch my kids pursue their dreams…just the idea of them was my dream all along.

As moms we are there *for* our kids and *with* our kids; we cry *with* them, cry *for* them, and cry *about* them because we have this opportunity that no one else has. We get to see their history unfold from the moment they take their first breath and every moment in between. We carried them and loved them in a way no one else could, or understood for that matter. We protected them from the moment they were alive in our tummies, waited for their movements, waited for their arrival, and treasured that first moment of pure heaven when we looked at their tiny faces and fell in love even more than we knew was humanly possible. We are their witnesses, their storytellers, and, most of all, their touchstones.

This is why I say it's an honor to be a mom; I hold their past, their present, and their future with one hand, and I hold on to the guidance and wisdom of God, my divine compass, with the other. He is the only One who loves them more than me…they are *His* first. God so graciously gave me this forever, because forever started when a doctor said, "You're going to have a baby." That doctor never told me that I was going to experience a love that cannot be articulated, or a bond that cannot be broken, or a heart so full of gratitude for a chance to have the title, wear the label, and have the most beloved name of all…*mom*.

I love the sound of that name as much today as when I first heard my daughter and son babble it. I love it as much as when it was sweetly whispered as *mommy* from the lips of my little toddlers. I love it as much as when I heard my daughter say *mom* on the other end of a phone line from college or when my son is calling it to get my attention. They may just be saying mom, but to me they are speaking volumes. What they say, what they ask, and what they need can be summed up in the unspoken...that name. Imperfect as I am, they still know that *mom* will be there to do, to listen, to try to fix, to encourage, to help, and to love—and to love regardless, I might add. We are blessed to *be* these blessings, to *have* these blessings, and I don't take it lightly...these are moments, these are lives, these are lifetimes, and we get to see it all! Do I get a lot of pats on the back, kudos, and tons of thank-yous? Maybe not, although I get plenty, but I don't really need them anyway...you see, the pleasure has been all mine.

SOMETHING'S MISSING

I WROTE THIS AT 2:00 a.m. after a sleepless night...so come along and shuffle around with me!

I can't sleep! I have shuffled around the house looking for things to do. My dear husband made scrambled eggs and left the kitchen a scrambled mess! I cleaned up the mess, did some laundry, and ironed a bit. I love to clean, do laundry, and ironing (which may be odd, but I find it therapeutic). I've watched *The Believer's Voice of Victory* (as I usually do every night at 11:30) with the ever-amazing Kenneth and Gloria Copeland. I am rereading *Hinds' Feet on High Places* but can't seem to concentrate.[1] Hmm...what's up? I try to pray...and all I can say is, "Lord, I miss my daughter."

My son is asleep. He fills my life in ways I could never describe. He is so sweet and just told me today how lucky he was to have me for a mom. I THINK I'M THE LUCKY ONE! When we are going about the day, our routine, and the busyness of it, I do OK. But when everything is quiet and everyone is asleep, then it becomes obvious...something's missing—or should I say, *someone*.

"Not a creature is stirring, not even a mouse" (I hope!). Everyone is where they should be: son in bed, husband in bed, cat in bed beside son, and all four dogs in bed! I walked down the hall and looked into Ashton's room—her *empty* room. I don't know why I chose to torture myself this way! I turned on the light and looked at her bed, which was made, but she wasn't in it. How many nights had I watched her and her brother as they slept? From those nervous first nights when I had to make sure they were still breathing, to the ones where they had been sick and looked so pitiful, or the ones where they looked like angels so peacefully unaware and innocent. I just sighed and stared at that empty bed. No little girl with her stuffed bear, no teenager with her cell phone inches away and the TV still on, not even the college girl home for a visit. I gazed around her room where she had crates packed with all of her high school memorabilia. She had decided that it was time to put all of those things away, so her walls are bare, the shelves cleared out, leaving just a few necessities here and there. Yes, something's definitely missing.

I started to get choked up and turned around to leave. Did God feel this way when His Son left to fulfill His purpose on the earth? I get that this is a part of life that we as parents can't avoid. I am happy that she is well on her way to fulfilling God's design and purpose for her adult life (really, I promise!), and I have peace in this time, as well. I just miss my daughter—plain and simple. I decided to shuffle back to my room, get under the covers, and contemplate. My choices were: never come out from under the covers, try to go to sleep, cry quietly (although loud wailing wouldn't wake my husband up!), or I could meditate on the Lord. Well, I chose the latter, and He came to me in His faithfulness, as always. He saw me and felt my sadness and longing, so of course He was there. "Although something is missing and someone is missing...*I am never missing.*" Wow, I know that He is always with us, but I never looked at it as *He is never missing.* He is never absent from us, our situations, and our needs. It's a completely different perspective for me, but it continues to emphasize the boundless love of our heavenly Father. Well, this was too good to keep to myself, so I had to write about it. I grabbed my laptop, started to type, and realized I was still missing Ashton. But I knew I wasn't alone, and nothing now...was missing.

HEART CRY

I REMEMBER WATCHING THE film *Temple Grandin* on DVD. I encourage anyone who can to watch it. Temple Grandin is a heroic figure in the autism community. She is a renowned speaker and author, and, yes, I've read every one of her books. Her book *Emergence: Labeled Autistic* was the first book I found on the subject shortly after Austin's diagnosis. At the time resources were sparse, and I found myself at the library pouring through diagnostic manuals when I stumbled upon this book. It was written from an autistic point of view, and it gave me the first bit of insight into my child's world. I could discuss this topic for pages. Persons with autism are mislabeled and misunderstood. They think differently and are some of the most brilliant minds on the planet. It's widely believed that Albert Einstein was autistic, and history can confirm that. I could try to explain the science of it all, but that's not what's important. Temple Grandin says, "I am different, not less." Hearing that phrase was a defining moment for me, and the significance of it was striking.

A doctor once told me that Austin had *vulnerabilities*, to which I replied, "Don't we all; we're just better at masking ours, aren't we?" Who gets to say what *normal* is anyway? Many autistic people refer to us as *neurotypical* and see us as those who are disadvantaged! I have to admit that I love that! Having lived with my son and witnessed how gifted he is and how amazing his mind is, I have to agree. His challenges are different from mine, but we *both* have challenges. His abilities are different from mine, but we *both* have abilities. His value and contribution are different from mine, but we *both* have value and make a contribution. Regardless of the hardships, or how they present themselves in our lives, all of us have a place at the King's table. We have something to offer humanity, and we have something to offer God's kingdom. *We are different, but not less!*

After Austin watched the movie, we discussed parts of it. I asked, "How did that make you feel?"

He replied tearfully, "Like I am finally not alone." Oh, my heart! Even though the message of the film was so positive and uplifting, his words felt like a bucket of cold water in the face. His dad and I call times like these *"cold-water moments."* Austin was actually relieved, but to a mom, it just plain hurt. No mom wants her child to hurt or struggle or feel different. I kept hearing those words *different, but not less.* This should become the heart cry of the church!

If we could ever embrace one another for whom God made us and stop the competition and judgment, how much stronger would we be. If we could offer understanding and acceptance, along with help and assistance, we could really be the family that God intended. If we could unify under the banner of true brotherly love, we could fulfill the Great Commission; *e pluribus unum*—"out of many, one."

Austin has taught me more than any sermon, or volumes of books could, for that matter. His lessons have been about life, love, understanding, patience, and choosing words carefully. He has shown me what it's like to have the purest of hearts and to see the good in everyone and, thereby, to want the best for them. He embodies the scripture "In whom there is no guile" (John 1:47, DARBY). Well, he embodies many scriptures, because he embodies the life of Christ, and he does because he is...different. He is different, just like his Savior; He was different too. Yes, we crucify people, in one way or another, for being different. But I hear this anthem, a heart cry, if you will—"We are different, but not less." All of us have a place at the King's table, and all of us get preferred or special seating if we make our reservations in advance.

RANDOM THOUGHTS
on a ROAD TRIP

I FONDLY REMEMBER BEING in the backseat of the car on a road trip with the guys—son and husband. We were en route to visit Ashton at college...so many thoughts were running through my mind that I had to jot down a few as we were driving:

Austin is in the front seat so he can control the radio. He loves eighties music...did I really dance to this stuff? Did I think I looked good with my enormous permed hair and giant bangs? (There was an art to doing big bangs with Rave hairspray, by the way.) You know what they say, "The bigger the hair, the closer to God!"

Travel with *some* guys is interesting (Austin not included). They take way longer to get ready, make several trips back into the house for things that they forgot, get hungry more, notice the oddest things, and complain about traffic, the cost of gas, disrepair of roads, and all other drivers.

Me—I had my list, was packed and ready in an hour, packed coolers, checked the guys' bags, loaded the car with all of the above (including one dog), and still waited on my husband, who forgot his glasses, his special pillows, his vitamins, and then changed to comfy shoes...waited some more. Pulled out of driveway—and guess what? Yes, you're right, he forgot something else! Waited some more...

We're taking Ashton's puppy back to her, which is currently doing gymnastics from seat to seat....I don't want a side trip to the vet.

The backseat is not too comfy—both guys have very long legs, and it is cramped back here!

Isn't it interesting how you can remember the words to a song that you haven't heard in years? Currently singing with Paul McCartney, "Maybe I'm Amazed." By the way, I used to have a huge crush on him, and I remember singing this song at the campfire at church camp...odd choice for church camp song. Oh, well, we also sang "We Are One in the Spirit." It was the Jesus movement, and we thought we were hippies at the ripe old age of thirteen. I wore my peace sign necklace to prove it.

I am Snow White, traveling with Sleepy and Grumpy—husband gets sleepy when he drives, and son is grumpy since the dog keeps jumping on him. Think I'll call the dog Dopey.

One thing I love about Ohio...I can still see and hear tractors. It's planting season—may God bless our farmers.

Just passed a fabulous outlet center, but naturally the guys would rather abandon the car and walk to our destination than shop...no fun.

Now, singing to Michael Jackson, and of course, I know every word—remembering all the guys back in the day who tried to dance like him, wore one glove and a red jacket...uh, they didn't succeed.

There are a lot of semitrucks on the road...that would be a hard job. Besides, where would we be without them? A big thanks to all of you!

The dog finally went to sleep...thank You, Jesus!

By the way, Jesus, please don't let my husband fall asleep...he is nodding a bit.

Now my son has switched to the nineties station—I don't know these songs since I was busy raising little ones then...who had time for the radio? I do know all the songs from *Barney* though.

Just passed a Keebler semi with chocolate chip cookies painted on the side...I wish I had some since I'm currently on the "everything tastes like dirt" diet.

Oops, husband woke up to scold drivers going too slow in the fast lane...in case you were wondering, he *is* the only human who knows how to drive.

Now he is giving us a crash course in nature—the life of the coyote...why do I need to know this? At least he's awake, but now I wish I *was* asleep.

They have no idea that they've inspired me to write about them...not sure if I'll tell.

Ahh, the open highway...sun shining, lovely scenery, but no Diet Coke in sight...starting to panic.

Just passed a Dip-n-Dots truck—I love those. If we pass a Diet Coke truck, I'm rolling the window down and asking for one.

Guys don't want to stop...why are they in charge? Maybe I need to pull the carsick routine.

Dog woke up...oh, no, the jumping has commenced...

Finally we stopped, and now husband can't find his exit...not this again. I already wrote about this subject and can't take another "99 Bottles of Beer on the Wall" by Austin.

We are now on the road again, and I have my pop, which is hard to drink with Speed Racer at the wheel...angels, get on your helmets and help!

Wish you could see and hear these guys singing Celine Dion...if only I had this recorded, I could definitely make some serious cash from bribery!

Austin's air guitar to Bon Jovi is priceless; plus he's wearing his Ray Ban shades...he's the coolest.

A word of wisdom to anyone who rides in the car with my husband: be prayed up, have your sins forgiven, and be ready...it's scary, seriously scary.

The grass is turning greener, the trees and flowers are budding...spring is in the air, and I love it.

We're almost there, and *now* the dog decides to fall asleep...it figures...

We arrived safely, and I will kiss the ground when I get out.

Day 2: It's been fun and memorable, especially when I went chasing Ashton's puppy across a parking lot in front of several college students...not one of my prouder moments.

Embarrassed kids with the aforementioned chase scene...*ahh*, I call that payback.

Seeing daughter so happy in her element and so *grown up* was surreal but satisfying.

Sadly, time to go...check-out is in thirty minutes.

Guess who is not ready? I've been up, got breakfast for everyone, packed, ready, loaded car, and even took a ride with Austin on the luggage cart...still waiting...waiting...

The little inn on campus is really cute and even has a porch swing. The kids and I are swinging...and waiting...and waiting some more.

Said our good-byes, wishing it would be easy; still not used to life without my daughter in our house...I've adjusted, though my heart protests daily.

Back on the road, and going to read to pass the time; son asleep, husband listening to news, traffic is heavy, and so is my heart.

Life and its cycles find me staring out the window wishing to understand this *letting go* deal; I don't remember signing *that* dotted line.

Home...thankful for every minute of the trip (well, maybe not *every* minute), realizing that time is precious, people are precious, life is precious...and Jesus, knowing You is most precious of all.

Road trip:
    Gas—$64
    Food—$76
    College education—I don't even want to know
    Time with those I love—*priceless*

THE HAIR BOW

HAT'S WITH THESE milestones, and why are there so many of them? I wrote this while preparing for a big one in a parent's life a few years ago.

Well, this is one of those moments. If parenting was a career consideration, this would be a time one might be looking into semi-retirement. Our daughter is graduating from college this weekend, actually on her birthday. She said her degree was the best gift ever, but I know when I see her in her cap and gown, I may think differently. Without a doubt, all else aside, along with her brother, *she* is the best gift.

I know when she's walking in the processional it'll be hard for me not to think of her twenty-two years ago. She came into the world in the afternoon and will walk out of the same world she has known all her life—all in a matter of minutes and with one piece of paper that says so.

I made a book of college memories for her and ended it with a letter from me. May I share from it? "The often-quoted movie line, 'You *had* me at hello,' was perfect for *that* story. For *my* story, you *had* me at 'Mrs. Parsley, the test is positive, and you're going to have a baby!'"

My book for her went on to share some mushy, emotional, and particularly personal stories, and then drew this conclusion: "*You had me at hello, and you had me at these last four years of good-byes. My little baby whom I loved, more than my next breath, grew up and took my breath away.*"

I was at the store with my daughter yesterday, and she was wearing her hair up with a headband that had a big bow. She was browsing around some counters, and I just stared. I remembered her hair that way many times before. On her first birthday she wore a big bow. And I could see it as if I were watching a video. I just stared and watched and wondered why I was so emotional. I was happy when she left high school because it was exciting for her to be out of the *bubble*, as we call it. I was anxious for her to have the chance to be Ashton, and not Ashton Parsley—Rod Parsley's daughter. I knew it was her time to be judged on her own merits and form her identity apart from us. I was sad she was leaving home, but my happiness for her eclipsed all melancholy moments of mine.

There she was with that bow—my little girl grown up and her own person. We sat at lunch as she discussed her favorite works of American literature and her favorite classes and professors. I was *interested* at how *interesting* I was finding her conversation. Then she talked about her brother as she reassured me that she would be home for the summer, and he would be fine now that "Sissy" was home. I smiled through tears because that darn bow was symbolizing my inner conflict! Were we just playing tea party, or was my daughter really graduating from college?

Letting go is obviously not easy for me! I know the deal that parents are to *give their children roots and wings*. But this is what I told her: "My arms held you first...before anyone else, so maybe you can understand why moments and momentous occasions are so emotional. Every moment is just one more tug out of my arms and into the arms of what is to come."

So tomorrow, as she walks with all the other graduates in her cap and gown...it's just one more tug. The bow will be gone, and soon she'll stroll into the arms of what awaits her young life. But my arms will never be too far, my hands will always fold for prayer, and my love—well...it's the kind that movies are made of.

MOMENTS *and* MEMORIES

ONE DAY I was discussing how we need to embrace every moment as the gift that God intended. I realize that every day I'm making memories for someone—good ones or bad ones. I certainly want to make lasting memories that reflect my love and God's love in me. I have succeeded and failed at this endeavor...haven't we all? Memories can serve us as lessons in what to do or what not to do, what to be or what not to be. They can also provide a link to the past, which creates traditions and customs that keep family and cultural legacies alive.

In my family many of the most heartwarming memories of my childhood came at the hands and heart of my beloved grandma. She went to heaven thirty years ago, but her smile, her words, and her love are living in the hearts of all of us. If I could be like anyone, I'd choose her. She epitomized unconditional love and the life of Jesus walked out in human form. Her life was simple but pure. She came to America at Ellis Island as a young girl at eighteen, after a customary arranged marriage to my grandfather. She was from Belgrade, Yugoslavia, and came, as she described it, to a country that was free and could give them a better life. She was courageous and hopeful in the face of the adversarial circumstances that lay ahead. Nonetheless, she built a life that included loving five grand-daughters who she claimed were perfect! We were the lucky ones, for in our eyes, she was the perfect one.

Every time I see her photo, I miss her. I thought of how she enriched our lives and how I see her character reflected in each of us. What a blessing to know that someone loved you more than anything...no matter what. Her life was her family; she didn't seek the typical trappings of success but ended up with the best life anyway—a lesson learned, no doubt. *It doesn't take stuff, things, power, position, attention, or the like to be successful. Too often this costs a family instead of building it.* Once again, "love builds the house," as the saying goes.

I started thinking of so many of my favorite memories; I could write a book since there are so many, but here are a few:

Her voice—she spoke with a heavy accent with very broken English, but it was musical.

The smell of her freshly baked bread covering her kitchen table—we'd always peek under the cloth waiting for it to be ready!

Seeing her in her apron and bonnet when we'd walk into her house.

Knowing that when we crossed the field to her house from ours, she'd drop everything she was doing to visit with us.

Listening to her, Grandpa, my uncle, and my dad have conversations in Serbian—I thought all families did this! Sadly I only know a few words and phrases.

Walking past her lilac tree to her back porch or picking peonies from her front yard—these are my two favorite flowers to this day.

Playing a game she taught my sisters and me called *Penny*—I think she made it up as a way to give us money!

Listening to her scold my dad if he scolded us—"You not talk to my girls like that, Otskie!"—we loved it! We knew we got by with a lot at her house! (Funny how my dad listened to her too!)

Watching her brush her long hair and then braid it into a bun with hairpins and hair combs that we would later play with.

Spending the night at her house—we got backrubs before bed, and then she woke us up singing *Revelry* and saying, "It's time for pannycakes!"

Looking out my window to see her and my grandpa working in the garden—complete with straw hats!

Remembering how she clipped the ads for the Billy Graham TV crusades and taped them above her sewing machine.

Watching her and my grandpa dance to music on the *Lawrence Welk Show*.

Remembering how she helped me learn to cook—she was an amazing cook and baker.

Watching her sew, knit, and crochet the most beautiful things.

Playing dress up with her pocketbooks, shoes, aprons, and bonnets

Still seeing her, arms folded, smiling and laughing as she watched us play—pure joy for her *and* for us.

Going into a storage area where she would show us items in a trunk from the "Old Country" and tell us such interesting stories.

Sitting at her table where she let my sisters and I have coffee or, should I say, sugar with a dash of coffee!

Her speech to all of our high school boyfriends when she would meet them—Julie and Jenny, I know you can recite this! "You lucky boy, my girl is perfect, she is good, she can cook, clean, she not go to bars, she is beautiful, she smart, you lucky." *Ahh*, who doesn't need to hear that?!

How she'd tell us if Prince Charles could meet us, he'd marry us! Again, who doesn't want to hear that?!

Her smile—she had a twinkle in her eye that was unforgettable…so was she.

Well, I am flooded with memories and emotion and could continue for pages upon pages. I hope I somehow captured the essence of what my grandma brought to our lives. Her life was a beautiful story, and we each have pages from it—words and moments layering the beauty of God's love as she wove a lasting legacy. It's not only a lasting legacy but also a lasting lesson. What she came to America seeking, she found—but we were the ones who got the better life in the long run. It's lovely to remember God's richest blessings. It's a way of saying, in the immortal words of Bob Hope, "Thanks for the memories."

RAISE YOUR GLASS

I'VE ALWAYS SAID that I don't see the glass half empty or half full...I'm just happy to have a glass at all! I was thinking today that I could count my friends on one hand. Don't feel sorry for me because honestly, if you have a few good friends, you're a rich person. We may know a lot of people, but true friends are the ones you can call in the middle of the night, and they'll come running. In my case my few friends can find me next door whining, or a few others at our rare but long lunches, covering every topic imaginable. When I count my blessings, I'm so thankful they're on the list!

It's a job hazard. Ministry affords you many wonderful people to be around but few friends. Coworkers seem to come and go and move around a lot, as do many congregation members. There are those who love like family, and I am so grateful for them...you have no idea. Some of the greatest people I've ever had the honor to meet sit in the pews of our church and provide living examples to me as well as others.

That said, I've never thought of myself as lonely, isolated, or without many friends. Aside from the obvious gifts of my husband and two amazing kids, I have a glass! That glass happens to be what God gave me and I've known my entire life. Case in point, I was sitting in a salon with hair color on my head (yes, covering the gray), and the stylist asked me why I was laughing. I replied, "I've been texting both of my sisters; they are my best friends." I guess that said a lot in just a few words, or did it?

How could I describe the joy and friendship my sisters bring me? We've shared everything over the years. We started with sharing time, rooms, clothes, the phone, and secrets. To date we've shared milestones, heartache, tragedy, weddings, babies, big moments, little moments, funny moments, common interests, and secrets. We have our own language, our own inside jokes, and our own *happy places*. They've come to my rescue, and I've run to theirs...without question or hesitation because that's what best friends do. I know many people who have sisters, but not all are friends. I guess I hit the jackpot.

We argued as kids, just like everyone. We fought over all the things I listed—rooms, clothes, the phone, and other stupid stuff. My mom would always say, "One day, when you're older, all of you will be best friends."

Wow, the faces we'd make when she said that! We'd always reply with the usual, "I'm moving as far away as I can get," or "There's no way I'm having a thing to do with her; are you kidding?!" As much as it pains me to say it…my mom was right. No kid wants to admit that all those parental lectures were true!

Actually, I'm happy she was right and that we stayed close and grew even closer when we didn't live together. I guess we realized that the bond we had was worth strengthening and holding tightly onto. I know that for me, *no one* could take the place of my two wonderful sisters. To think that they know all my faults, all my past failings, and still love me makes them priceless. Whenever I see a text message with the names Julie or Jenny, my heart leaps a bit. It's usually something in just our language, but it always makes me smile or laugh. To be honest, it always makes me want to raise my glass, with our beverage of choice—Diet Coke!

In so doing, I think of what I have and, moreover, *whom* I have. When I raise that glass, I can see what the Lord has done and what He has given me, and this I know for sure: "My cup runneth over."

RANDOM THOUGHTS
on the HOLIDAYS

AMIDST THE HUSTLE and bustle of Christmas and holiday seasons past and present, could I let an opportunity pass without random thoughts on the matter? I think not...

Where *did* all my letters to Santa go?

No driving school prepares you for the department store parking lots, mall lots, or worst of all...the dreaded parking garage during the holiday season. Not even a NASCAR or stunt driver could compete with women on a mission.

That said, I've been nearly run over, sworn at, gestured at, and have dueled for a spot like a cowboy from the Old West.

Christmas shopping is an art and requires the mind-reading skills of a psychic. Do they have this? Will they like it? Will they need it or want it? Where's Cleo when you need her?! (Disclaimer—No, I don't believe in psychics!)

Why was it that my kids always wanted the hot-ticket item for that year—the Tickle-Me Elmo, Tamagotchis, Beanie Babies, Furby, Grand Champion Barbie, and the first-ever Nintendo DS? Of course, there were always limited supplies, so leaving with a rain check was the ultimate bummer.

To get aforementioned gifts, I've shamelessly stood in lines in subzero temperatures, been awake at dawn, waited in parking lots, stared down other moms, and all but offered to sell blood plasma to get those items.

By the way, my stare says, "Look, lady, I was raised in redneck country, and I will wrestle you to the ground for this Furby, so don't push me. Where I'm from, we believe in God and guns!"

I always loved how we'd stay up putting toys together on Christmas Eve, fall into bed at 3:00 a.m., and at 4:00 a.m. two little kids were so excited they couldn't sleep and were ready to be up opening presents.

I knew they'd grown up when I waited for them to wake up...and waited...and waited. Who was the kid then?

I was always concerned that there were leftover parts and screws when my husband put things together...handy with tools he is not.

He never needed to read directions on toy assembly either. Is this in a man's DNA or what...seriously?

Hmm...selling my blood plasma, now there's an idea. I'll keep that in mind when grandkids are in the picture.

I love football, but honestly, there is a bowl game for everyone by every company these days. Back in my day we had the Rose Bowl, the Cotton Bowl, the Orange Bowl, and the Sugar Bowl. Now there are bowl games named for everything: tortilla chips, macaroni n' cheese, cell phones, car repair, pizza, and even poinsettias...*sigh*. Is anything pure anymore?

I have photos of my kids with Santa. I recall jumping up and down behind the mall photographer trying to get a smile out of terrified-looking faces...I am left asking myself, "Why, just why?"

Speaking of Santa, may God forgive me for telling my kids that if they misbehaved, I'd call Santa's Naughty Hotline.

Of course, my darling little daughter retorted, "Never mind, I asked Santa for coal, and I'll be happy with that!" I never got one up on her...never.

I remember my son crying when the Disney Christmas parade was over on TV. He and his sister were sitting atop her Barbie playhouse. Yes, the one that Dad assembled with parts left over...I was nervous.

I also remember how his sister comforted him…that's never stopped.

He still has the scar above his lip where he cut himself trying to open his Elmo package. I remember I was getting his bath ready, and he found scissors, and I almost passed out. The scar has faded, but the guilt, however, is still fresh.

One of the low points of the holiday is seeing grown men dressed as elves. What makes a man put on tights and say this is worth the humiliation?

I might also add that not all mall Santas look or act the part. I realize it may be a drag holding terrified kids whose crazy moms are forcing the experience and jumping up and down behind the photographer (yes, I mean me), but you're paid to be jolly and roly-poly—not skinny, crabby, or slightly drunk.

How many of us have used the "I'm one of Santa's helpers" routine when kids caught us with their gifts before Christmas Eve?

I remember, as a little girl, crying on a Christmas Eve because we didn't have snow, and I thought Santa couldn't land the sleigh. My dad told me that Santa had special blades on the sleigh for grass landings…good one!

Rudolph the Red-Nosed Reindeer was the first show that I ever saw in color. My sisters and I will never forget my dad carrying in a color TV on Christmas Eve, which back then was a huge sacrifice. We were so thrilled, and I can still see his smile.

The toys on the Island of Misfit Toys were always my favorites. They're the ones I would've wanted anyway, since misfits make up the best toy box…I think misfits are God's favorites too.

If I were a Christmas dessert, I'd be a fruitcake—perhaps a little fruity, a tad nutty, shoved to the side for the flashier ones (sniff!), and certainly misunderstood. Guess that's better than being a cut-out cookie.

There's nothing *too* tacky at Christmas time. It's the time for the Christmas sweaters that light up, the earrings that look like giant ornaments, Santa hats, reindeer ears, Rudolph noses, and outrageous lawn decorations…it's all good 'cause it's a party!

Yes, that also includes dogs dressed as elves, Santa, Rudolph, little Christmas trees, or Max from *The Grinch*…obnoxious is acceptable this time of year!

I can say that because I bought shirts for my dogs that look like candy canes…at the dollar section of Target, I might add.

Speaking of Target, it's where I went with my daughter to buy her first Christmas tree and decorations for her college apartment…I didn't ask Santa for this, and that lump of coal felt like it was in my throat.

Austin and I have a tradition of watching certain Christmas videos together: *Annabelle's Wish*, Opus and Bill in *A Wish for Wings that Work*, *A Charlie Brown Christmas*, *Rudolph*, and others—we're sentimental and always get choked up no matter how many times we've seen them. (We just finished Opus…tears.)

We have traditions that are special and timeless…not fancy or formal, just simple and enduring.

If we take a peek, we can find the gifts of Christmases long ago, of recent memory, currently, and even those to come. Our expectations may be one thing, and what shows up may be another, but there is still joy to be found. *Just the thought of the hope that Mary held in her arms is gift enough. Hmm…enough is an insufficient word. Everything* is more like it. He came, He gave, and He was and is…everything.

Glory to God in the highest heaven, and on earth peace to men on whom his favor rests.

—LUKE 2:14

Although the world is full of suffering, it is full also of the overcoming of it.[1]

—HELEN KELLER

Part 6

BUILT *for the* BATTLE—
STRUGGLES *and* HARDSHIPS

OES ANYONE HAVE a trouble-free life? If you do, please let me in on your secret! Actually, I know that life is filled with promises, and some of those we may not like. We are the sum total of what we've been through...good and bad.

Life's difficulties leave a lasting impression that molds us into the people we are. While we're going through tough times, we need the gentle voice of God reminding us that while we were promised trials and tribulations, we were promised a Savior to be with us along the way.

He battled death, hell, and the grave and won...I think we're in good company!

> And after you have suffered a little while, the God of all grace [Who imparts all blessing and favor], Who has called you to His [own] eternal glory in Christ Jesus, will Himself complete and make you what you ought to be, establish and ground you securely, and strengthen, and settle you.
>
> —1 PETER 5:10, AMP

LIFE, INTERRUPTED

WHAT HAPPENS WHEN things don't go according to plan? What do I do when I *don't* expect the unexpected? How do I respond when life gets interrupted? To some people, going with the flow is easy. For me, going with *my* flow is easy! I like things done on schedule, according to my plan and according to my calendar. I plan my week, even with others' plans in mind, and find comfort in doing so. However, after years of unpredictability habitually creeping its way into my world, I've had to learn to adjust my sails. This boat called *My Life* doesn't always sail on calm waters. Instead the ride can be unsettling and turbulent, tossing not only my plans overboard but also my lunch! As I sail, my skies present a myriad of different hues. There are beautiful sunrises and beginnings that can only be matched by sunsets so stunning one knows they can only be the creation of the *original artist* named God. The sun shines and warms as the moon lights and guides. The clouds shade and give me a chance to dream. I bask in the glorious concept of life as I know it or, dare I say, life as I *want* it.

Then it happens...the thunder rolls, the lightning crashes, the clouds gather their fury, and the storm rudely interrupts my tranquility. My serenity is replaced by panic as I breathlessly seek shelter. I look to the elements to inform me, my eyes on the tempestuous skies...not on the shelter that lies ahead. I've concluded this one thing: I am Peter (well, in a few ways). In Matthew 14, when Peter saw Jesus walking on the water, Jesus called for him to come. Peter had *a word* from Jesus, and that's all he needed. He got out of the boat but was then distracted by the winds and became afraid. Peter cried, "Lord, save me!" Been there, done that, said that. Jesus instantly reached out and grabbed Peter, saying, "O you of little faith, why did you doubt?" (Matt. 14:31, NKJV). In other words, Jesus was essentially telling him this: "When I told you to come, I was planning on taking care of you until you reached Me. When you took your eyes of faith off of Me and became fearful, you began to sink. Regardless, I was there to hold you and save you."

We may have *our* plans, but God always has one of *His* own. *In every plan there is a purpose, and part of that purpose is the stark realization of what every experience can bring to our lives.* Peter wouldn't have known how good the arms of Jesus felt had he not begun to sink. I have this to say: at least he got out of the boat and tried! It reminds me of the words to one of my favorite songs, "Fix You": "But if you never try you'll never know just what you're worth."[1] *We can't learn to get up until first we know how it feels to fall down.* We don't know how it feels to be right until we've been wrong. It's been said often, but we don't appreciate the mountaintop until we've been in the valley. *Peace doesn't seem tangible until we've experienced unrest.*

Life *does* get interrupted, and things don't always go our way, but if we can adjust our sails, we won't capsize. Jesus has called us to come to Him, and He will take care of us all the while. He knows the seas will be variable, and we'll discover uncharted waters. However, if we have faith in His protective provision, we'll find the shelter of His loving arms as He holds us and calms the winds that have led us off course. Peter got back in the boat, but this time Jesus got in with him, and they went to the other side as Jesus had planned all along. His plan is always better, and, even in sinking, we can learn there's something new on the horizon. I remember something I once read: "You can't cry *Abba* until first you cry *uncle!*" Life pushes us beyond our human limits, but it pushes us right into the arms of a limitless God.

IT'S *the* LITTLE THINGS

T HE OTHER DAY my husband called and was so excited. He'd stopped at a little country store and found some caramel corn, which he liked, and then chased it with a grape soda! I teased him by saying it was funny or sad, depending on how you look at it, that a good snack was the highlight of his day! He replied, "Well, it's the little things." I immediately responded that he'd just given me an idea for the journal. Sometimes it *really* is the little things that make a moment special or add happiness to our day. Maybe it's as simple as a grape soda and some caramel corn, but it creates a feel-good moment nonetheless. Here are some of the little things that make me smile:

- Apple cider and caramel apples in the fall

- Seeing pumpkins on porches (also in the fall)

- Hot chocolate—Bob Evans (popular Midwestern restaurant) has the very best...*yum!*

- A fuzzy blanket on a chilly day (good book optional)

- The sound of wind through trees—Al Gore would be proud...I'm a bit of a tree-hugger

- Scented candles—especially pumpkin vanilla featured in the fall

- Pretty much anything that has to do with the fall in Ohio—just wish it was longer

- A good Diet Coke (like you didn't know that one!)

+ Popcorn at the movies—it doesn't taste the same anywhere else (chased with a Diet Coke, of course)

+ Early mornings—it's the newness and the promise of it all

+ Lying in bed during a thunderstorm—I feel so safe…*He is my shelter* in every other storm

+ Sitting on a porch swing and daydreaming (ask my sisters, I've always done this!)

+ The feeling I get when I walk into the Longaberger Homestead (again, ask my sisters!)

+ UGGS—God bless whoever invented these comfy slippers, shoes, and boots…I call them *hugs for feet!*

+ The sound of a fountain or waterfall and water in general—*I still feel small when I stand beside the ocean!*

+ Sitting by a fire or fireplace—so cozy

+ Still seeing my kids asleep—*sigh*…so angelic

+ Driving alone with good music—I do sing along…sadly this embarrasses my kids

+ Embarrassing my kids…it's a sport to me (especially during the teen years)

+ Text messages that are sweet or make me laugh from my peeps (hubby, kids, sisters, nieces, nephews, and friends)

+ OK, I hate to admit it, but a guilty pleasure…*People* magazine (I really do read it for the articles!)

- Flannel—I never met anything flannel that I didn't like—maybe not my best look, but who cares?!

- Laughter—the feeling of it, the sight of it, and the sound of it..."A merry heart does good" (Prov. 17:22, NKJV).

I guess that scripture really explains my list. I've described my favorite things before, but they're on a grander scale. These are just some of the little things that give me moments of simple pleasure. These moments are called *blessings*, and blessings are simply the favor and love of God. I think He gives us appreciation for these little distractions. After a tiring day my flannel, my UGGS slippers, and *ahh*...a good Diet Coke can take my mind off pressures and problems. My list makes me merry, even for a moment, and *it does me good!*

Now it's your turn...think of some of your little things. It does a heart good!

A CARTOON LIFE

WHAT IF LIFE could be like a cartoon, and we could choose the one we'd like to be in? I've sat through some boring programs, boring sermons, boring movies, and boring speeches that I wished would end. I even went to an outdoor docudrama and thought it would *never* end. I've been to concerts that were snoozers, unless it was with my daughter, during her *NSYNC years, where all I heard was two hours of prepubescent high-pitched screaming! I attended plays for college credit where students were overacting, went to ballets that I never understood, and poetry readings where would-be poets were trying too hard to be abstract and deep. The common thread in all this monotony...I wanted it to end; whatever it was, I just wanted it to be OVER!

Do I not enjoy culture? Well...I do enjoy *what* I enjoy, and some culture I appreciate and love. If you enjoy something, you don't care how long it goes. Most guys probably wish there were twelve innings of baseball and six quarters of football. (We ladies don't care as long as they're watching somewhere else!) Funny, I never get bored at the mall or a craft mall, and I could stay for hours at the Longaberger Homestead!

One Christmas I remember dragging my husband to *The Nutcracker* when the kids were small because I thought it might be a nice family tradition...wrong! He didn't last long and spent the rest of the night at the snack bar....that was the last time he was invited! In his words, "Men who go hunting do not go to ballets!"

Wouldn't it be great if we could treat life like a play or movie? We could choose the parts we wanted and our costars too! We'd perform a certain way, have everyone else follow the script, and no ad libs or rewrites would be permitted. We'd have wardrobe, hair and makeup, assistants, drivers, and catered dinners. All we'd have to do is show up, know our lines, perform, and get paid millions. Well, it's not that easy. Directors, costars, and other people on the set make that life difficult too, and then others critique your work anyway. I guess that life may not be so grand, after all.

How about the life of a cartoon? In thirty-minute episodes all of life's ups and downs are funny and still get solved. I think I'd choose to be Jane Jetson! She never ages and has a tiny waist! She has a robot maid and buttons she pushes that get her ready on a daily basis. I don't think she has a job, but she flies around in her little aircraft and dishes out her lines and wisdom just like the evening meal. She is annoyed by her husband, George, but look at Wilma and Betty in *The Flintstones*! These women certainly were the brains of these operations! Jane had technology on her side, while poor Betty and Wilma were using prehistoric animals as household appliances! Forget that; I want the robots!

If Jane were on Twitter, I guess she'd say, "Another day seeing the kids off to school and George off to Spacely Sprockets." What *did* she do all day? I guess maybe cartoon life would be boring too! At least there's always a happy ending. Don't all of us want that?

No matter how we get there, and who our supporting cast of players may be, we will have the theatrical experience. A good play has a good theme—it has conflict, conflict resolution, colorful characters, a protagonist, an antagonist, a climactic scene, and a conclusion that ties it all together.

I went to a community theater play with Austin, who had a classmate performing. The play was so good that I didn't want it to end; I got lost in the story and caught up in the characters. The final scene left me in tears because it had a wonderfully moving message of how love changes us. That message has stayed with me.

Jesus performed the scene of all scenes...on an old rugged cross. He didn't ask for the starring role, and even asked to be replaced, but He did as His Father asked. Though the drama was intense and unfolded in a way the human mind cannot comprehend— there was a death and the ending was bloody, but it was still going to be a happy one. There were two more sequels, and *the last scene ended with an empty tomb but not one empty promise.* Just like the aforementioned play, that final scene left me in tears because it had a wonderfully moving message of how love changes us. Likewise that message has stayed with me.

So, I guess I don't want the cartoon life or the movie star life. I would like my life to be easier, but when I think of that old rugged cross where He suffered and died, how can I complain? He gave me my happy ending, after all. Just like every fairy tale I've ever read, *her Prince had finally come, and together they lived happily ever after.* The End.

I WISH I WAS *a* KID AGAIN

I HAVE DECIDED THAT being a grown-up has a lot of advantages, but it has its drawbacks as well. It's days like this when I wish I was in kindergarten having story time with milk and cookies and naptime afterward. I wouldn't have to be around big people with their big problems and their big agendas. I could lose myself in Dr. Seuss-land, where life is simple and characters are colorful and don't have to make sense. OK, I realize this may be idealistic and rather immature, but being in touch with one's inner child is supposed to be a good thing, right? Well, mine wants to scream, "Stop the world; I want to get off!" I want to run out to recess and swing as high as I can, then climb the monkey bars and sit atop pretending I am the queen of the playground, the way I used to! Why do we wish to grow up so fast and leave our carefree days behind? I think I will imagine that I am a kid again and go outside to the lush green meadow by my beloved grandma's house and look up to the clouds as I lie there. I will imagine that God and I have story time, and He is reading to me something that sounds a lot like my favorite Dr. Seuss. It would go something like this:

> So here we are, My little lamb, it's Me, it's Me, the God I
> am.
> I hear you don't like the world BIG, you do not like it in a
> box,
> You do not like it wearing socks, you do not like it with PB
> and jam,
> I'm listening, says God I am.
>
> I hear you don't like the people big, you do not like them
> with green hair,
> You do not like them anywhere, you do not like them
> screaming loud,
> You do not like them preened and proud, your list is long,
> My fax has jammed,

But I'm still reading, says God I am.

Now I see you don't like life so grown, it's not always fun
       just on your own,
You do not like it when there's bills, you think they should
       come wearing frills,
You don't like them in your mail, they make you want to cry
       and wail.
I hear you and I understand, I really do, says God I am.

There's more, there's more, the list still goes, there's more
       dislikes, there's lots more woes?
There is more complaining and pouting too? There's more of
       what these grown-ups do?
Like lie and cheat and hurt your heart, and zig and zag your
       life apart,
And do it with a knife and smile, and leave you crying all the
       while,
And do so without a care, of how they caught you unaware,
My, but this is getting dreary, no wonder you have gotten
       weary.
I hear you still, I really do, but it's *My* turn to talk to you.

You will always be My little one, though growing up is not
       so fun,
But I am with you every minute, take Me along so I am in it,
And it may not be all that bad if you just let Me be your Dad,
To teach and love but dry your tears, chase away monsters
       and calm your fears,
Because I love you and you're not alone, I am here now that
       you are grown,
I've always been your biggest fan,
Love,
Yours truly,
God I am

Sometimes the kid in us needs to have a temper tantrum and
let God kiss our boo-boos and bandage our bruises. That's the
balm of Gilead that Jesus talks about and so lovingly applies to our
wounds. *We do not have to be justified in our hurts—just hurting*

alone qualifies us for His ministry to you and me. He is there to teach us instead of lecture when we have ill feelings. *Our feelings are ill and need healing, and a big dose of His love is the best prescription.* Life in God can have childlike simplicity even when the characters are colorful and don't make sense—it still makes for a good story time.

CLOAK *and* DAGGER

THIS IS NOT the beginning of a mystery...or is it? It's always been a mystery to me *why* people hurt each other and *how* they do so. I'm not saying that I've never hurt anyone, be it consciously or unconsciously, but I hate knowing if I do. Some people are so thoughtless, careless, and entitled that hurting another is like taking a drink of water—just part of the daily routine.

By now you're probably saying, "Wow, she must be angry with someone, and this is going to be a rant." Nope. Of course, I've been hurt, as all of us have. However, let's say this—being hurt does not make me *or you* a victim. I refuse that title because it leads to excuses and self-pity. I prefer to say that I'm a survivor. A survivor searches for ways to endure the challenges ahead *and* behind, to brave the elements, to remain. When we're hurt, it's time to put on the gear and grab the ropes and shoes, because we're going mountain climbing!

Our feelings and emotions, when wounded, can become a large obstacle that gets in the way of our peace and healing. We obsess over conversations or relive a confrontation because the hurt clouds our thinking and abducts our peace of mind. Furthermore, when we ache with battered and bruised hearts, we have a natural tendency to focus on our injuries and the pain. When we ignore doctor's orders, so to speak, we refuse the treatment plan as well. Soon enough the wound becomes a cancer that leaves our relationships on life support and gasping for breath...do we pull the plug or not?

If we rehearse how we were hurt, what was done or said, we will knock someone out of the way to get to be the one to pull the plug! On the other hand, we can follow orders—beginning with a word we don't want to hear...*forgiveness*. Let's be honest; we'd rather hear the word *revenge*! Sorry, but we don't get automated options! We don't get choices: Press one if you'd like fire and brimstone to rain down from heaven on your foe! Press two if you'd like their actions recorded for the evening newscast! Press three if you'd like an instant replay of the conversation so you can say all the things you wished you'd said! Press four if you think you were justified and they deserve whatever is coming to them!

Guess what?! No choices, no system, it's all or nothing! *Forgiveness is a cornerstone of our Christianity when we claim to be followers of Christ the Redeemer.* He forgave our sins while *dying* on a cross, yet we can't manage to muster up the grace to do likewise?! We get no justification, no excuses, nothing but one word— FORGIVE. When we say it, mean it, and allow our hearts to express unconditional love, the healing balm begins to flow.

Now, I have been tough on those of us mountain-climbing over the heap of hurt, but now it's time to talk to the offender. Let's admit it—we are all guilty as charged! Words are so powerful because we were created in the image of God; what He has, we can have. His words created the heavens and the earth. He didn't use His hands, build a bulldozer and a crane, or use a set of tools...HE SPOKE! The power of words can frame a world...they can frame *your* world. Words are creative. We can create good things and bad things, hurt or healing, damage or disaster relief.

What we *cannot* do is allow ourselves to be seduced by current technology and hide behind a keyboard or a cell phone. The enemy has been successful in getting us to wear our cloaks, conceal our true identities, and throw our daggers. Often we can do so in 140 characters or less. Matthew chapters 5 and 18 tell us to go to our brother if we've offended him and initiate forgiveness regardless of whether we are the offender *or* the offendee. Jesus reconciled us, so we're to do the same with others—reconciliation starts with forgiveness.

Hiding behind a keyboard empowers us. I know...um, because I've done it! I recall my husband and myself getting into a text war of words. Then we talked and made an agreement never to text in anger again, and we haven't. Years ago we agreed not to write letters, notes, or anything; we confront issues by TALKING (sometimes loudly!). I don't quite have the nerve to say things in a conversation that I would in a written message. Besides that, it's impossible to interpret the tone or true intent in written messages—it's too easy to read something inadvertent between the lines.

Plain and simple, words create. Plain and simple, words hurt. They wound in a way that Proverbs 18:7–8 describes vividly: "A fool's mouth is his undoing, and his lips are a snare to his soul. The words of a gossip are like choice morsels; they go down to a man's inmost parts." *We can remember hurtful words way more than compliments because they intrude on a soul and spirit meant for communion with God and the purity of His love.* Our job is to express that love to one another. Our crime is feeling entitled to say what we feel with the cavalier attitude to *let the chips fall where they may.* The lesson—keep the chips and don't take the gamble.

UNBROKEN

WHAT DOES A person do when she watches her child suffer? Where does she put that kind of pain? I have felt helpless, but never, never hopeless. I have run the gamut of emotions and felt every feeling to the extent humanly possible, I guess. What remains unchanged is still unbroken...my hope is unbroken. I have known what it means to be broken. I have had broken dreams, broken plans, broken finances, broken relationships, broken health, and a broken heart, but I have never had my hope broken. It may be all I feel that I have, but... *I have hope.*

I don't want to seem melodramatic because I also have perspective. Although I've suffered a miscarriage, I have not had the pain of burying a child or the full scope of that grief. I have not held the hand of my child as he or she went through a terminal illness and the painful procedures that accompany that. I've not watched my child homeless or hungry. I've not watched my child go off to war and not come home. Nonetheless, pain is relative, and pain still hurts.

As I've recently watched my son agonize for nearly two weeks, I've cried out to God to give that anguish to me; it would be easier that way. My wise friend always tells me to look for the miracle in every day and in every hardship. To take away pain is to take away growth, but honestly, I'd much rather have my son's pain than watch it and not be able to fix it. Can't growth come any other way? Can't God make life easier? Do I care about life lessons at a time like this? I just want God to *make it all better* and to do it now! I've had a few of these temper tantrums with God, but I've never been angry with Him. His love and mercy prevail even in the darkest hours. My prayer, beyond the obvious, is to know Him as my son does. As he was struggling through the night with this torment, he began to cry. He cried out to God and spoke words from the depths of a heart that knows God on a level few do. "Please, my sweet Lord, my sweet Father, help me." At that point I buried my head in a pillow and lost all composure. Who loves through all that pain and still calls God "my sweet Father"?

Many Christians pout and get mad at God when things don't go their way, never giving Him a chance simply to love. That, my dear brothers and sisters, is called *immaturity* and *insolence*. I heard a lady a few weeks ago who said she was mad at God. I could clearly see how God had done the miraculous, but she was totally missing it by fixating on circumstances. Was all this trouble God's fault? Isn't He referred to as "blameless" for a reason? Some people don't know real tragedy and heartache, so they mountain-climb over molehills. We have to step back and examine where God's hand moves in situations. It may not be moving the way we want it, or fast enough, but it is moving nonetheless…we just have to look, and furthermore, we have to trust. There will come a time when you will experience *the breaking* and thank Him through it. Soon, thereafter, will come the giving, and the Job season will be over.

My human mind does not understand what my son is going through and why. It's like a bad dream, so surreal. We have done *what* we know, but we rely on *whom* we know…HE NEVER FAILS! Because He lives and loves, my hope is unbroken. That hope was built when I knelt at an altar and surrendered *the hopeless* for *the hopeful*. This hymn says it all:

> My hope is built on nothing less
> Than Jesus' blood and righteousness;
> I dare not trust the sweetest frame,
> But wholly lean on Jesus' name.
>
> When darkness veils His lovely face,
> I rest on His unchanging grace;
> In every high and stormy gale,
> My anchor holds within the veil.
>
> His oath, His covenant, His blood
> Support me in the whelming flood;
> When all around my soul gives way,
> He then is all my hope and stay.
>
> When He shall come with trumpet sound,
> Oh, may I then in Him be found,

Dressed in His righteousness alone,
Faultless to stand before the throne.

On Christ, the solid Rock, I stand;
All other ground is sinking sand,
All other ground is sinking sand.[1]

ROAD RAGE

Have you ever had one of those days that left you in total frustration? On a recent trip I experienced just that! We were driving down the busy California freeway where traffic, to midwesterners like me, is crazy! My dear husband (and I use the word *dear* loosely here!) was driving and assuring all of us he knew where he was going...red flag! Our drive time, coming and going, should've taken about forty-five minutes but ended up being four hours! May I add that these were four of the longest hours ever—childbirth was easier. There was one traffic jam after another, so Rod kept taking alternate routes while still telling us he knew where he was going.

Now, I have a question, and it's one of the mysteries of the universe: What is it with men and directions? Is it a secret sin that women aren't aware of to ask for directions?! Is it a male ego thing? Is it an admission of weakness that you may need help after all? What is it—I HAVE TO KNOW! When I get to heaven, I'm going to ask God about this, but I think He'll answer, "This is why I created women, because Adam needed help getting around the garden and wouldn't ask Me for directions!" I am certain that the GPS navigation systems were created by a frustrated woman, but this day not even technology could help me. We had a GPS in the car and on our cell phones, but my dear hubby would not use them—*he knew where we were*...really?!

By hour two I wanted to scream out the window. I tried deep breaths, praying, more deep breaths, and nothing worked! Austin started singing, "99 Bottles of Beer on the Wall"! I know it's not too spiritual, but desperate times call for desperate measures! And yes, he got through the entire song! I wanted to take one of those bottles and knock it over my husband's head by hour three! I realize that it's *way* too human to feel this utter frustration, but at least I'm honest. Finally, after a tearful plea, we called for an address and loaded the GPS...thank You, God! Not long after, much to my amazement, we arrived back at our hotel, and I wanted to kiss the ground and never get in a car again—especially with, well, you know! I was spent! Then my niece, Amy, said, "Well, the main thing is that we are all safe, and God could've kept us from an accident—you never know." *Hmm…* now I feel bad! Those freeways are dangerous, we were lost, and native Californians drive a lot faster than we Ohioans!

Could it be that there was something from this madness that I could be thankful for? Was the hand of God at work? I remembered our pastor, Dr. Lester Sumrall, always saying that *any delay is of God*. That truth has kept me from so much frustration in the past, but I just didn't think about it this time. God's plan is never on our time table because He knows that we need to, "Let patience have its perfect work, that you may be perfect and complete, lacking nothing" (James 1:4, NKJV). Another translation says it this way: "For you know that when your faith is tested, your endurance has a chance to grow. So let it grow, for when your endurance is fully developed, you will be perfect and complete, needing nothing" (vv. 3–4, NLT). As I've said, *to take away pain is to take away growth*. I guess I must be fifty feet tall!

I know our road trip was an insignificant thing in comparison to real-life challenges, and I've had my share, but *God will use anything to remind us and teach us*. He used a talking donkey (and no, I'm not referring to my husband here!) in the story of Balaam (Num. 22:22–41). Interestingly enough, Balaam was being stubborn and resisting the direction of the Lord. God sent an angel to block the road, but only the donkey could see the angel and stopped. Finally, after Balaam beat the donkey (in a fit of road rage perhaps), God gave it the ability to speak. I can definitely identify with the donkey's first words, "What did I do to deserve this?" I love God's unconventional teaching methods! For me, He used a busy freeway, a typical male, and even "99 Bottles of Beer on the Wall"—but I got it! Lesson learned and message heard…loud and clear!

I'VE BEEN TRYING, for the last few days, to come up with some amusing random thoughts. I figured that I haven't done any for a while, and it was time for a little levity. I have since drawn this conclusion...I don't feel very funny! What's the deal? Has life been too heavy? Have I become too serious? Am I "weary in well-doing" even though the Scriptures tell me not to be? Are the gray skies of our long Ohio winters getting to me? Am I a curmudgeon who has lost her sense of humor? Is the well dry or the attic of my brain filled with cobwebs? As my head collapses on my keyboard, I realize I have no answers, but one realization...I need to laugh.

I saw a guy jogging today in orange spandex. I said to myself, "What's this, the ballet? No men should wear spandex, especially in orange, for goodness sake! It's not midnight; it's 9:00 a.m., and I can see you, unfortunately!" I chuckled but did not laugh. Speaking of men wearing what they shouldn't, Austin was laughing about a YouTube clip of Richard Simmons. He laughed so hard I thought he was choking, but me...again, just a chuckle. It was hilarious, but I just didn't feel it, I guess. *Ho hum!* Now that I'm conscious of it, I'm worried. I need to laugh. What's the prescription for that? I think of the scripture where it says, "A merry heart does good, like medicine" (Prov. 17:22, NKJV). Maybe what I need is a merry heart, not just a good laugh. So I ask myself, "Self, what's keeping your heart from being merry?" I read on in verse 22, "...but a broken spirit dries the bones" (NKJV). Immediately another scripture came to mind: "Let us lay aside every weight, and the sin which doth so easily beset us, and let us run with patience the race that is set before us" (Heb. 12:1, KJV). I guess I have my answer! I have been beset!

Other translations of that scripture relate being beset to being entangled, surrounded, or plagued by the cares of this world. Having said that, I realized what a rush I'd been in lately, or maybe more like a dense fog. I *never* took time to laugh. If I wasn't running off somewhere, my mind surely was. I started imagining what it's like when I drive in fog; I lose visibility and sense of direction. I have to rely on the lines on the road and do so little by little. I may not see my destination, but I know I'll get there if I'm patient. *Hmm*...I think I just described faith.

I have been running the race, but I have been carrying an elephant on my back, so to speak, and I'm not getting very far. Ask any doctor, and he'll tell you that extra weight is bad for the bones. Bad or brittle bones are easily broken. From that I understand one way we can become broken; the cares of this world were never ours to carry. God knew the weight would be too much, so He sent a Savior to bear our burdens. That leads me to ask: Have I just been saying words? Do I cast my cares on the Lord then take them back? And...the answer is yes! It's easy to do, but it's better to leave them where they belong! As I always say, *easy is not always better!*

It doesn't take a genius to know that sin is weight and excess baggage that our lives do not need. David said, "I have hidden your word in my heart that I might not sin against you" (Ps. 119:11). More Word means less sin. More of God means less of this world. Less worry means more joy...it's just that simple! I guess God has the best weight-loss plan around!

THE FIVE Ws and the H

I'T'S IN TIMES like these that I find myself questioning. I'm not sure whom I'm even asking—maybe myself, maybe God, maybe no one...I'm just not sure. I guess that's the issue after all...I'm not sure. I tell myself that God is sure when I am not. I tell myself a lot of things—we have many conversations, just me, myself, and I!

I know me. I like to understand and know all the reasons behind situations. I like answers. When there are no answers, it requires trust, and I don't often like that! I'd rather know a timeline, a plan, a beginning and an end. God doesn't always work that way. We have to walk by faith, and often it's blind faith. We can't see where we're going, so we have to hold on to our guide, who knows the way and can see what we can't. That takes faith. Meanwhile, trust and hope are the critical components in that walk of faith. There is a difference in *knowing* and *having answers. Faith knows God. Trust takes hope by the hand and informs the soul that "all is well" because God is in control.*

There have been many times where it felt like everyone had abandoned ship, and I was on the *Titanic* scrambling for a life-boat! Even when we're lost at sea in the darkest hour, Jesus still walks on water and bids us to come. That is the God I know. He never leaves us, even in our most painful moments when nothing makes sense and we just want to run away from it all. We have all these feelings, and we don't know where to put them. He is our burden bearer and tells us simply what to do. "Casting the whole of your care [all your anxieties, all your worries, all your concerns, once and for all] on Him, for He cares for you affectionately and cares about you watchfully" (1 Pet. 5:7, AMP). Well, I guess that about covers it!

In Psalm 55:22 we are told to: "Cast your burden on the Lord [releasing the weight of it] and He will sustain you; He will never allow the [consistently] righteous to be moved (made to slip, fall or fail)" (AMP). The key is to be consistently righteous, which means in right standing with God. That comes with knowing and, then, doing. Ecclesiastes 12:13–14 (AMP) has been my passage to live by for years. It answers the *who, what, when, where, why,* and *how* of my life and all the mysteries that have come with it.

> All has been heard; the end of the matter is: Fear God [revere and worship Him, knowing that He is] and keep His commandments, for this is the whole of man [the full, original purpose of his creation, the object of God's providence, the root of character, the foundation of all happiness, the adjustment to all inharmonious circumstances and conditions under the sun] and the whole [duty] for every man. For God shall bring every work into judgment, with every secret thing, whether it is good or evil.

That not only says it all—it answers it all.

THE ONE THING

As I struggled searching for an answer, a shred of truth, or a glimmer of hope in a seemingly dismal set of circumstances, I began to pray. Well, I began to cry and whine, to be honest. But God, a patient and loving Father, still answered as I listened to the prayer of a dear saint. She was praying a poetic and powerful prayer, and then she said one phrase that hit me like lightning, *"You're the one thing..."*

As I continued driving, I began to think on that one phrase and therein found what I was looking for. *I started taking inventory of how that one phrase could answer every tear-filled moment.*

- When I can't rely on anything, He is the *one thing* that is constant.

- When no one can give me an answer, He is the *one thing* that has them all.

- When I am suffering in silence, He is the *one thing* that hears my every cry.

- When I feel desperate and hopeless, He is the *one thing* that finds hope a home.

- When I am rejected and called "less than," He is the *one thing* that calls me His own.

- When I am broken and in disrepair, He is the *one thing* that has purposed my completion.

- When I am low on courage, He is the *one thing* that is perpetually heroic.

+ When my dreams are deflated, He is the *one thing* that breathes life into them once again.

+ When I am afraid, He is the *one thing* that answers fear with peace.

+ When I am troubled and overwhelmed, He is the *one thing* that calms the storm-tossed waters.

+ When I am absent from the minds of others, He is the *one thing* that's always thinking of me.

+ When I feel unloved and unlovely, He is the *one thing* that gives me "beauty for ashes."

+ When I cannot seem to put one foot in front of the other, He is the *one thing* that is "the glory and the lifter of my head."

He has "borne our grief and carried our sorrows," and because of that I trust Him. I trust Him *ruthlessly*, as Brennan Manning says,[1] and I believe...in this "*one thing*."

ADDITIONAL RANDOM
THOUGHTS

MY FIRST RANDOM thought today is that my brain feels scattered and nothing makes a cohesive point whatsoever! So here we go with some additional observations on life...random as they may be!

I want to be somewhere and be surprised by a flash mob.

I do not want to dance in a flash mob, however, unless my kids could be there and be totally humiliated.

Speaking of such, when did I cease being a superhero supermom and become an elderly embarrassment?

Nonetheless, I love the look of sheer wide-eyed horror when I do embarrass my kids (which doesn't take much, I might add). I don't really know why, I just do...*mwah-ha-ha!*

It fascinates me that fast-food places can do so many things to a hamburger and a chicken sandwich—but no matter what they do, it's still just a fast-food hamburger, not a gourmet experience.

On that note, we have a new chicken fast-food place in our town, and it's such an attraction that police have to direct traffic...*hmm*, what does that say about our town?

Not that I'm a snob or anything; I've been there...twice.

It's summer and time for amusement parks. I used to wait in line for two hours to ride the roller coaster; now I just have to wake up.

I have stared at the computer cursor blinking at me. I am struggling to write as it hypnotizes me and taunts me, saying, "Your mind is blank, and so is your paper"...blink, blink, blink. Is it called a *cursor* for a reason?

Got to spend time with my great-niece who is ten months old. No matter what she does, we think it's perfect, completely brilliant, and absolutely adorable. I have spent the day marveling at her, snapping pictures, and talking baby talk to everyone.

Having said that, I wonder if babies wonder why we talk like that and just want to tell us, "What's with the baby talk? You really can speak in a normal tone."

I admit it; I talk to my dogs in the same voice. I'm sure they wonder the same thing.

Summer brings out some interesting fashions, or lack thereof. Look, ladies, to everything there is a season, and a time to give up shorts and tank tops. If you can pull it off, more power to ya!

On that note, guys, please never wear a Speedo unless you're in the Olympics.

Also while I'm at it, black socks are for dress pants only. Never wear with shorts and Rockports or tennis shoes. It's only acceptable if you drive a Buick and have retired to Florida.

I wish kids today would put down the cell phones and electronics, stay outside until dusk, lie in the cool grass, catch fireflies, ride bikes, play tag, and drink from a water hose when they're thirsty. I just described the majority of my summer activities as a kid, and I never remember being bored.

Blink...blink...blink.

My sisters and I would ride our bikes, sit on this bridge, throw rocks in the creek, and just daydream...I can picture it as if it was yesterday.

Do kids even daydream anymore, or is there an app for that?

Adding to the "what kids of today are missing out on" list—drive-in movies. Nothing like wearing your pajamas, popping your own popcorn, filling the thermos with Kool-Aid, and piling into the car with pillows, blankets, sisters, and parents…I couldn't wait for dusk.

I also remember that my mom was pretty clever in getting us to stay quiet through the movie. She told us that anything we said could be heard over the speaker in the window and would go to every other car. I totally bought that one, and getting me to hush was not an easy task.

I also remember falling into the toilet at the drive-in. I was little, and my parents wrapped me in a blanket and hung my PJ bottoms out the window to dry…fun times!

More blinking—try again tomorrow…I'm sleepy, I'm sleepy, I'm sleepy, I'm sleepy!

Ever notice that the more you try to hurry, the more random, crazy things happen? You rip your jacket, lose a pet, lose a cell phone, a kid throws up, car won't start, get in construction traffic, or so often in my case, there's a train on my way to church…really! (My husband never believes this.)

I don't see dandelions as weeds; how can a yellow flower be a nuisance?

I wonder if parents will be judged for all the little white lies we have to tell our kids. Will God just see it as a means of survival? Things like: Chuck E. Cheese is closed today because Chuck E. needs a rest. I am just one of Santa's helpers because he is so busy. If you roll your eyes at me, they'll stay like that. Thunder is just God bowling with the angels. Of course, they have bowling in heaven; they have all sports there. The dog went to stay at this farm where he could recover and play with other dogs that have been injured. The fish are sleeping; that's why they float at the top of the water. The bird flew away to reunite with his family—and the list goes on and on and on.

Random as life is, there is something someone said to me recently that I just loved: "God is sure." Think about it! No matter what random, typical, atypical, or oddly distracting things happen to us in one day, God is sure! Life changes in ways that challenge us, but we have a blessed assurance that we can depend on a God who "changes not." I'm just glad that when I strap in for the roller-coaster ride, I have a constant companion…hands up!

Who looks outside, dreams.
Who looks inside, awakes.[1]

—CARL JUNG

Part 7

CAREFUL CONSIDERATIONS—
REFLECTIONS *and* MEDITATIONS

WHAT ARE YOU thinking? Before we speak, we have to think! Therein lies the answer to most of the mysteries of the universe—mankind needs to think! Careful consideration gives our expression a chance to be seasoned with wisdom and grace.

Selah is a word found numerous times in the Bible, especially in the Psalms. It means, "to pause and think calmly on that." When we pause, we keep eternity in full focus, and in so doing it changes our behavior and our course of action. The key is to be still, and that's another challenge for me! But I'm reminded of the scripture, "Be still, and know that I am God" (Ps. 46:10). When we stop and take a good look, we also can see all that God *has* done and *is* doing for us, and then we stay encouraged.

He can make our dreams come true, but…we have to *dream* before He can *do*.

> For the rest, brethren, whatever is true, whatever is worthy of reverence and is honorable and seemly, whatever is just, whatever is pure, whatever is lovely and lovable, whatever is kind and winsome and gracious, if there is any virtue and excellence, if there is anything worthy of praise, think on and weigh and take account of these things [fix your minds on them].
>
> —PHILIPPIANS 4:8, AMP

MY MEANING *of* SUCCESS

WHILE DRIVING HOME late one evening, we were listening to the radio, and singer Mark Lowry quoted someone saying, "The first half of our lives is dedicated to being successful, and the second half is dedicated to being significant." Oprah calls this an "aha moment." I thought about this the rest of the drive home, and I have continued to ponder this statement ever since. The question I kept asking myself was, "What is success anyway?"

I guess many would define success as having wealth, power, position, and fame. Others might add family, happiness, and health to that list. Is success, like beauty, in the eye of the beholder and a totally subjective opinion? My answer would be an unequivocal and emphatic YES! Beyond that, *my* definition of success *is* about being significant. What would the world be like if we were as dedicated to being significant as we were to being successful? What would our families be like if we created *moments in our occasions* instead of *momentous occasions* that we could brag about as we "keep up with the Joneses"? Who are these Jones people anyway, and why do they have the power to keep everyone striving to be something or to live up to some predetermined ideal? I just want to shout from the middle of Times Square, "Where are all of you going, and why are you killing yourselves to get there? RELAX!"

I heard June Carter Cash once say that all she was trying to do was *matter*. Yes, another aha moment! Can we just take time to stop and think and matter? Can we get off the hamster wheel and stop chasing the pellet long enough to be significant in our lives and in the lives of those around us? Can we do the hardest thing of all and truly *let go and let God* so that we could actually do what Hebrews 12:1 (KJV) says and "lay aside every weight, and the sin which doth so easily beset us" (and I'm preachin' to myself here)?

My son, Austin, bought me a calendar of quotes for moms that I love and read daily. I love quotes, quote books, and all things quotes! This particular quote said, "My mother wasn't just interesting—she was *interested*." *Aha* again! I realized that wanting to matter, being significant, and being interested had one common denominator—they take the focus from ourselves and place it on others. If we can take our eyes off of *ME, MYSELF,* and *I* long enough, we can actually see others…we can notice. If we *really* notice, then the chain reaction begins; we *can* be our brother's keeper, we *can* matter, and we *can* be significant.

My favorite Mother Teresa quote is: "There are no great things, just small things done with great love." I think we can all agree that her life was one that epitomized what significance truly means. Her success cannot be equated with material gain, but certainly by a wealth of riches of another kind—the *best* kind. This was the kind of great love that Jesus talked about throughout the Gospels and the kind that He lived and that He was…all the way to the cross. Because you and I…*we mattered.*

CASUAL OBSERVER

I WAS ON A search for inspiration. I had a bad case of writer's block, which I attributed to a lack of sleep and caffeine. I don't require much sleep, but I do require copious amounts of caffeine! I am trying to cut down and be healthier, but my brain is protesting! So I decided to look for inspiration at the local Barnes and Noble bookstore (*noble* stands for "my noble sanctuary"). However, I found myself distracted by people ordering their lattes, a table of teenage girls giggling over boys, a staffer stocking shelves, some jazz music, and the sound of the blender making coffee drinks. Normally I can tune all of these sounds out, but not that day. So here's the story as I wrote it that day!

I remember telling my children about the wonders of the library and bookstore. I described that every book they could see began with an idea, a dream, and some inspiration. I'm thinking about here I am surrounded by brilliance in one form or another and yet... nothing. I could write about Julia Child—her cookbooks are on a shelf next to me. She certainly had a colorful life and career. I could write about the table of girls who are talking (loudly, I might add) about their hair and cell phones. Oh, to have a life where that was important! Now they are actually discussing who can wink with both eyes... wow, I am concerned for our future! Across from me is an older man reading a comic. What's that about—does his wife not allow comics? Does he have to sneak and read *Superman* at the local bookstore? Next to me is a beleaguered young student with her laptop. Is she trying to work and is as distracted as I am with the MTV girls nearby? Oh no, now they have started on the iPods and music selections while trying to quote lines from songs... help me, Jesus! When did I become so old and serious?!

I wish I liked coffee, then I could just get an IV drip of caffeine. A girl just came by with chocolate chunk cookie samples— manna from heaven?! Just chatted with the friendly manager who knows me well (since I'm such a regular); I am really thinking I should have my own parking spot here. Could there be a more faithful customer? I think not! Back to the girls and a new topic—brainwashing in college. This should be good! Could *those* brains be washed? They are complaining about all the reading and writing in education today, and all I can say is *wow*, imagine that! What nerve that any college would ask a student to read or write when there are iPods to load, hair to fuss over, cell phones to update, and eyes to practice winking—who has the time?

Have I become a cynic? An old, stuffy bookworm who looks down her nose on the trivialities of youth? I guess I just don't want young people to miss out on the noticeable simplicity of life, the influence of books, and, well, intelligent thought and conversation. These children get to vote—help us, Jesus!

Maybe I need to ask comic guy what Superman would do in such a dilemma. If only I had X-ray vision to stare a hole into this overbearing group of the "Ya-Ya Sisterhood." Maybe then they'd whisper while some of us are trying to actually work *and* read—since we have been brainwashed and all!

Can I find a lesson in any of this? Maybe I am being harsh—is it their fault I am lacking caffeine and creativity? They have been oddly entertaining after all. Ah, I just chatted with one of our Harvest Prep students who is intelligent, is diligent, is musically gifted, and, to top it off, loves God. *Sigh.* There is hope for this generation, and I am taking this as a sign! Update—one girl is laughing as she describes how her grandparents locked her out of their house! Uh, I just want to add…"Honey, no wonder!" We old people like it quiet, and we already know if both our eyes can wink. We have been through enough *not* to find hair trauma a true crisis and only see cell phones as a necessary evil, not a lifeline more important than blood and breath.

Now a toddler is crying, and I want to join her! Has she seen her future and is sad that that's all there is? I guess comic guy has the right idea. In a world that often doesn't make sense, find an alternative. I did…when I was thirteen years old, I realized this world couldn't offer me everything I needed or wanted. *I knew that there was something more, and there had to be* Someone *who had it.* Even on days like this He still gives me inspiration, hope, and a love that never fails. By the way, He is *even* better than Superman…His name is Jesus.

IS CUPID STUPID?

PERHAPS THIS ISN'T the forum for venting or sounding off, but I'm going there anyway! Now that it's over, I just have to say it: I think Valentine's Day can be ridiculous. I know you hopeless romantics find me cynical and harsh, but it's how I feel, so you've been warned! I think it's adorable when children are little and you can make heart-shaped cookies, send valentines, and make special boxes to keep them in. I loved the little parties we did as kids, and I remember counting my valentines the same way I did my trick-or-treat candy. I also remember making the grandest valentine boxes for my kids, which had me in craft stores and up all hours trying to outdo the previous year. It's another holiday that's wonderful and innocent for kids, but it stops there for the most part...at least in my opinion!

I'm sure you're wondering why I'd choose to harp on this topic, but I can't tell you how many people I've heard say, "I hate Valentine's Day!" I've heard young girls, wives, husbands, and single women and men of all ages lament the woes of this day devoted to love and those enraptured by it. However, I walked into a store where all I saw were men at the flower counter and card section looking perplexed, worried, and anxious...no one was smiling.

It's a day of expectations—often *unrealized* expectations. Someone called it SAD, Singles Awareness Day, because it makes one all the more aware that they're single! For every happy girl in love there are a hundred sad ones, and for every happy wife there are a hundred pouting and muttering, "My husband is an unromantic bum." Beyond that, you'll find women happy with the traditional roses and candy, but others who are thinking, "Wow, flowers and candy? How original is this guy? Am I not worth a little more thought?" Moreover, for every packed restaurant with couples enjoying an overpriced meal, there are those of us who had Easy Mac alone in front of the TV. Aha! So you're thinking this is why I'm so grumpy! No, my husband didn't forget Valentine's Day, although I would have to be sure it's tattooed on his forehead, recorded on his phone, plastered on his calendar, and put on a Post-It note on his steering wheel...he's a busy guy! Anyway, I let him off the hook. I told him I don't need money spent on a day that was created by greeting card companies and has become so commercial and too predictable. There's no magic and mystery in a day that mandates you to give someone attention and to do so with pink and red hearts...where is the fun in that? Maybe for some it's a special day that gives you an opportunity to be original, creative, and full of surprises...I don't begrudge you or deny you.

I'm not totally cold and heartless! I've been to lovely Valentine's Day weddings and know of many who have had magical moments on such a holiday. I have marveled at some of the grand gestures that some have done for their sweetie. More often than not, however, are the many sad faces I see avoiding the overloaded Valentine aisle in the store. This day ends up leaving many with a lump in the throat and a bump on the heart. It is a day like many holidays, unfortunately, that becomes a nagging reminder of the love people want and don't have. It's Charlie Brown waiting for the little red-haired girl all over again! It begs the question, do we really believe in the fairy tale and the happily-ever-after? Or is Cinderella hanging out with the mice and doing chores while everyone else is at the ball more the reality? *Can we find contentment when feelings of happiness elude us?* Most of all, is another person the answer?

I have felt like the apostle Paul...but shipwrecked by love! How's that for melodrama?! I have also had to shake off a snake or two! But I am reminded of Paul's words, and they have been the Post-It note on my steering wheel of unhappiness many times.

> I know what it is to be in need, and I know what it is to have plenty. I have learned the secret of being content in any and every situation, whether well fed or hungry, whether living in plenty or in want. I can do everything through him who gives me strength.
>
> —PHILIPPIANS 4:12–13

So maybe it's a day where I find myself alone with my thoughts and some Easy Mac (the ultimate comfort food), but I know a secret...His secret. He strengthens me in any and all ways and *all* days too. He loves me, and it's a love that Cupid didn't bring. What unfailing love is this? A love that pierced His hands and then His heart is the same love that pierced my loneliness, my sadness, and my hopeless eternity. I feel like Cinderella; the glass slipper fit, and I believe in *that* "happily ever after."

JONI GOES *to the* DOCTOR

I REMEMBER READING A book to my kids to prepare them for doctor visits. They were always about a character going to see their doctor, such as *Big Bird Goes to the Doctor*, *Arthur Goes to the Doctor*, *Elmo Goes to the Doctor*, and so on—you get the idea. Well, the last two days have seen this character at the doctor for tests, exams, and what-have-you. Yes, Joni goes to the doctor. Joni hates to go to the doctor, and by the way, she hates when people refer to themselves in the third person too!

The first reason I don't like doctor visits is the wait—this wait wasn't so bad, but always bring a book, something to read, or a phone or person who can entertain you. These are *my* serious survival strategies!

The biggest reason I hate doctor visits is getting weighed. Why is this necessary? Why does a doctor's scale always weigh you heavier than the one at home? Why don't they let me get on and off, as I do at home, until I find a weight that I can deal with? And above all, why do they have to shout your weight so everyone can hear it? I am surprised that it doesn't go over an intercom, "Here's Joni's height and weight; calculate her ideal weight—there's a prize for you!" I am a pro at getting weighed, by the way. I wear light clothing, take off all jewelry, and, yes, make them wait while I take off shoes and anything else that can add extra ounces. I always ask for the customary two pounds for clothes, especially jeans, but never get it. I've tried telling them I have steel pins in joints or artificial parts that weigh more—whatever it takes, people! I jest, I'd never lie about this, but my driver's license might beg to differ.

Now my wonderful doctor has this newfangled machine that weighs everything—my worst nightmare. It prints out what every body part weighs...oh, the horror! Do I need to know what my head weighs, or my arm or leg? Furthermore, I have one leg that weighs more than the other...what's up with that? The way I see it, my torso alone is my ideal weight...this is not good. I was forlorn, dismayed, and maybe even a little choked up when I got my printout. I stared in utter disbelief, and then became terrified at the thought that this was on file somewhere! This is now my medical history...oh, no! Am I vain? I've always found myself delightfully self-deprecating. How could I ever take myself seriously knowing my flaws as I do? However, now some of my flaws were in a file folder somewhere for the world to see! That's certainly humbling...well, "pride goeth before a fall," I guess!

As if the scale from Satan wasn't torture enough, I had to do other tests. All were tolerable in comparison except two. One was the glucose tolerance test. They give you these when you're pregnant, and it consists of drinking some nasty stuff. Now I ask, it's been eighteen years since my last test, and no improvements on the drink yet? Again, what's up with that? You would think that with a Starbucks on every corner, with a thousand ways to get coffee, someone could come up with a better drink for these tests already! It was still disgusting, and I kept gagging it down little by little. When I was pregnant, I would tell myself that I was doing it for the baby—that was my motivation. Well, the only baby here was me—and I was a big one! They kept checking, and I kept sipping. I also kept looking for somewhere to pour it out, but no sink, no plant, no nothin'! Finally, I did it! Then the blood draw was done, which was followed with a major sugar rush. I was so dizzy and running into walls like a drunk. Maybe my one leg that weighs more than the other was throwing me off balance...who knows!

They took so many tubes of blood that I could've easily satisfied all those vampire kids in the Twilight movies! My last test was three hours long, and it came with a big shot and an IV and more blood. I really don't mind needles, but IVs seem to hurt...*waah!* It's too complicated to explain, but it does something to measure hormone levels, which helps keep me off the crazy train—you ladies understand what I mean! Besides, my husband and kids don't need to be passengers on that train, so whatever it takes, I'll do. (No comments, family!)

Now I sat in this room with a needle in my arm and then it hit...conviction. I thought of how impatient I was, how I just wanted out of there, how I got upset over a report on weight and drinking some yucky stuff. I wasn't a big baby; I was a big brat! Sitting in the room, even reading my Smith Wigglesworth book, I felt like a spoiled brat who took God's gift of health for granted. My doctor is a brilliant woman, and I trust her completely. Her staff is so amazing and so kind and helpful. They've taken a person who was really sick a few years ago and helped get her well again. Best of all, they're Christians, and her plan for me was God's plan for me. *Sigh*, when will I ever learn? A few years ago I wouldn't have cared what anyone did to me; I just wanted to be well. I got well, and now it matters? Shame on me! How soon we forget.

When God brings us out of something, we need to remember and integrate that growth into our lives as part of our worshipful service to Him. He is the God who brings us through the valley, but when we are on the mountaintop, we need to look down and think of where we've been and how we got there. As we go, as we think, as we act, we need to do so in humility, knowing it was God's grace that did it all. To Him be all the glory…and the credit!

His goodness overwhelmed me in that exam room. I told Him I was sorry for being bratty, and I thanked His holy name for all that He had done. I built a memorial in that room. For the last hour of that test I remembered how sick I was sitting in that same room two years ago, and I thought long and hard about where God had brought me. I was thankful, so thankful, and it took a trip to the doctor to remind me that God goes to the doctor too. What a character—what a God.

RANDOM THOUGHTS FROM
the STORAGE ROOM

I REMEMBER CLEANING OUT closets and tackling my storage room to get items for a church garage sale. I've purged those places many times in the last twenty years, but this time was different. At the time, my son had graduated, my daughter had turned twenty-one, and the remnants of the school years needed to go. This had been a painful and arduous process! I am sentimental but also practical. I always think I'll have use for something, so I have a hard time letting go of it. Well, I took a deep breath and dove into this project, many years in the making, and made some interesting discoveries along the way.

Yes, I am sentimental, and I have the *stuff* to prove it!

Exhibit A—my majorette boots from high school! Why do I have these? Do I plan on marching in a parade and twirling my baton anytime soon?

Exhibit B—in the same tub are many of my college papers. Speaking of antiques, they were typed on something few may remember—an electric typewriter! I can still see where I used white-out! Boy, do kids have it easy these days.

Exhibit C—tubs of the kids' clothes of various ages and sizes that I couldn't part with. Many are the dresses that look like the ones from those kiddie pageant shows. Ashton, I'm sorry I tortured you, but you definitely paid me back during the teen years.

Speaking of tubs, I love containers. I notice that I have containers for my containers; this seems to scream that I have a problem. I like being organized, which also means that The Container Store is quite heavenly, as is the container aisle at Target. Yes, I have a problem.

Speaking of Target, I love the dollar aisle too. I don't really need anything there, but it's filled with *stuff* I *might* have a use for...someday.

I've been looking through old photos with Austin, and we came across one of me in the eighties. Honestly, I marvel at how I got my hair that enormous. It's not a hairstyle but rather a work of art. I loved the eighties.

I finally admit it! I have way too many Longaberger baskets. Isn't the first step admitting you have a problem? Is there a "Basket Collectors Anonymous"? Please don't tell my husband, or he'll start one.

If your heart can be seen in your treasures, mine must be throwing kids' parties. I could honestly open my own party store. Interestingly enough, I've only thrown a handful of "big people" parties, so what does that say? *Hmm*...kids are *way* more fun.

A container of parent books—how to do everything, craft anything, discipline anything, plan and organize anything, and execute said plan, just to name a few. However, judging by the bookmarks, I was too busy parenting to read most of those parenting books.

Some of my stuff is just plain tacky and somewhat odd—I have football helmets that hold chips and dip, bowls that look like swimming pools, an aqua platter in the shape of a fish, and a taco holder that looks like a football field...yep, garage sale.

With all our travels over the years I have three shelves of luggage. There's a bag for any and every type of trip: overseas, under the sea, domestic, carry-on, road trip, hunting trip, camping trip, long trip, short trip, and two giant duffle bags that we call *the body bags*.

I found a container of the kids' schoolwork and refrigerator art that I've kept through the years. Should I choose a few pieces and discard the rest? Can I do that while imagining those little fingers that created this work with great effort and pride? The lid is going back on for now... I don't have the heart for it.

Ah, the container of Ashton's Barbie collection. She'd never take the dolls out of the box, which is odd when you think about it. I am staring at one of the Barbie dolls that happened to be the hot ticket for Christmas one year. I was one of *those* moms who waited in line before the store opened, clawed my way to the door, ran like the wind to the Barbie aisle, and shamefully jumped up and down when I conquered all others and got the goods. If only the theme from *Rocky* had been playing, the moment would've been complete.

Speaking of doing things I never thought I'd do... I also was desperate for the first Nintendo DS that Austin wanted for Christmas one year. I combed through every store, called people I knew all over the country, and finally resorted to eBay. Winning that bid was like winning the lottery, and seeing Austin's face when he opened it was like cashing the check. God moves mountains for us too.

Why do I have a box of Valentine cards? I have SpongeBob, Pokémon, Disney, Barbie, Looney Tunes, *NSYNC, and Spice Girls. There are no more Valentine parties where sweet little cards are exchanged. Actually, there is no more *NSYNC or Spice Girls either. I loved the nineties.

Easter box is next. I seem to buy Easter grass every year, and now I have a tub of it. Any clever ideas for Easter grass use? I could make bird nests, zany wigs, or line a hamster cage, but I don't have a hamster. If it were 1895, I could stuff a mattress or carpet the garage. Note to self: do not buy any more Easter grass from the dollar aisle at Target.

Fall decorations—what can I say? I love fall and obviously love craft shops as well. Time to get rid of the cutesy scarecrows, fake pumpkins, and well, lots of junk. I always threw a fall party for kids called the Hallelujah Party so they could dress up in costumes, have a bonfire and hayride, and get loads of candy. Kids are still *way* more fun.

Speaking of costumes, I came across *that* box, and between my son and daughter they've dressed up as Elvis, a fairy princess, Buzz Lightyear, Pocahontas, Captain John Smith, a ballerina, Jan Brady, Scooby-Doo, Fred Flintstone, Princess Jasmine, Aladdin, Ash Ketchum of *Pokémon*, Dexter of *Dexter's Laboratory*, Sandy from *Grease*, Molly from American Girl, and, OK...this is getting to be too much. I hear Barbra Streisand singing, "Memories, light the corners of my mind..."

She's still singing:

Misty water-colored memories
Of the way we were.
Scattered pictures
Of the smiles we left behind,
Smiles we gave to one another
For the way we were.[1]

I loved that movie...I loved the seventies.

Newlywed years, baby years, toddler years, elementary years, teenage years, high school years, college years...I've loved every year.

WHEN IT RAINS, IT FLOODS

THERE'S THE OLD saying, "When it rains, it pours." Beyond that, when it rains heavily for a sustained amount of time, flooding results. Welcome to my world! I would describe the climate of my life recently as monsoon weather. No umbrella will do in this kind of rain; you just have to run for cover.

I'm stating fact, not fear. It's been a tumultuous few weeks, but I have on my life jacket and am hangin' on! At some point I just have to laugh...what else is there to do? As I always say, "Life happens!" It's in those times that some well-meaning person always says the proverbial "When life hands you lemons, make lemonade." It's also in those times that I want to throw those lemons at the person who says that! I shake my head while complaining, "If they only knew what I had to deal with." Of course, I'm the only one in the world experiencing difficulty...poor, poor pitiful me! As if my whine-fest wasn't bad enough, in walks my son, complete with halo and a serving of guilt. He tells me he's reading the book I bought him (darn, that bookstore!), and it's an interactive guide to time with God. Here comes the guilt! He tells me that today's challenge is to go an entire day without complaining. He declares a fast—no complaining for one day! What?! *Heavy sigh*...I agree and accept the challenge.

Back to the flood—soon thereafter my husband came upstairs to inform me that the storage room had flooded, and part of the basement too. There stood Austin (halo and all), and I thought I better find some duct tape to keep my mouth shut. How was I going to make lemonade out of this? I had Noah's flood down there and couldn't say a word! Was I supposed to swim, do the backstroke, and look for the rainbows? I wanted to unleash my furor of frustration, but instead I just said, "Now the mystery is solved."

The frustration was over the fact that I'd been telling my dear husband for days that the water pressure was low and something had to be wrong. He kept saying he'd "look into it," so now he could "look into it" wearing swim goggles and scuba gear! Yet I stood there and just stared at him...speechless. Oh, believe me, I had lots of words I wanted to use, but I couldn't use them. A deal's a deal, and a fast is a fast. God was teaching me, and I didn't like it one bit!

All day long Austin kept asking me if I'd complained. I had so many opportunities and thought of all the comments I usually make when certain things crept up. I came to a harsh conclusion...I complain too much! I don't make the lemonade, because complaining that the lemons are sour is way more satisfying! It doesn't always have to be something I say; it can also be a thought or attitude. *Negativity always begins with a thought, and in my case, that thought makes its way out of the mouth at some point.* Most of the time I mutter to myself, but sour lemons are still sour lemons.

Complaining is a knee-jerk reaction. A reflex happens without thought or intention. When a doctor strikes my knee, I don't have to think or try; it thrusts forward all on its own. We don't have to try to be negative; that's easy. *Trying to be positive and disciplined takes effort.*

I learned something about myself—all from a flood, a book, a son, a fast, and a forgetful husband. Life has handed me lemons on more than one occasion, but making lemonade is too easy and predictable. I'll just count my lemons as opportunities to learn...*um*, even when I don't feel like a lesson. So maybe there's a flood, literally and figuratively, but this I know...where there's a flood, there's always an ark. I guess that means I don't get to float through life, but that's OK—*Have flippers and goggles, will travel,* or better yet, swim. I may run out of breath, but no matter what problems I wade through, God will *look into it.*

ESSENTIAL THINGS

ONE EVENING I was reading in my Amplified Bible when this poem fell out. I had placed it in there to share with our Valor College students in chapel. This poem is one of my favorites! I love the practicality of these very profound words, and given the current climate, I find them quite appropriate. The title, "Desiderata," is Latin for "essential things." It was written in 1920 by Max Ehrmann, but the words are as relevant as if written this year. The first line is a truth that I hold dear and is a beautiful sentiment that is necessary for all of us. I hope that you are inspired by these words that are so full of wisdom...a proverb for today.

DESIDERATA

Go placidly amid the noise and haste, and remember what
    peace there may be in silence.
As far as possible without surrender be on good terms with
    all persons.
Speak your truth quietly and clearly; and listen to others,
    even the dull and ignorant; they too have their story.
Avoid loud and aggressive persons, they are vexations to the
    spirit.
If you compare yourself with others, you may become vain
    and bitter;
for always there will be greater and lesser persons than
    yourself.

Enjoy your achievements as well as your plans.
Keep interested in your own career, however humble; it is a
    real possession in the changing fortunes of time.
Exercise caution in your business affairs; for the world is full
    of trickery.

But let this not blind you to what virtue there is; many
        persons strive for high ideals;
and everywhere life is full of heroism.

Be yourself.
Especially, do not feign affection.
Neither be cynical about love; for in the face of all aridity
        and disenchantment it is as perennial as the grass.

Take kindly the counsel of the years, gracefully
        surrendering the things of youth.
Nurture strength of spirit to shield you in sudden
        misfortune. But do not distress yourself with dark
        imaginings.
Many fears are born of fatigue and loneliness. Beyond a
        wholesome discipline, be gentle with yourself.

You are a child of the universe, no less than the trees and
        the stars;
you have a right to be here.
And whether or not it is clear to you, no doubt the universe
        is unfolding as it should.

Therefore be at peace with God, whatever you conceive
        Him to be,
and whatever your labors and aspirations, in the noisy
        confusion of life keep peace with your soul.
With all its sham, drudgery, and broken dreams, it is still a
        beautiful world. Be careful. Strive to be happy.[1]

                                        —MAX EHRMANN

As I read this, I am reminded how the apostle Paul ended many
of his letters with the words *grace and peace* or some variation of it.
This poem is a deep breath of peace wrapped up in the gift of grace.
"May the God of hope fill you with all joy and peace" (Rom. 15:13).
It is the perfect exclamation point!

> I pray that God, the source of hope, will fill you completely
> with joy and peace because you trust in him. Then you will

overflow with confident hope through the power of the Holy Spirit.

—ROMANS 15:13, NLT

THE LIBRARY CARD

THERE ARE DEFINING moments in a person's life; we all know that. More importantly, there are defining moments in the life of a child that shape who that child is...forever. My parents raised my sisters and me to be avid readers and to love books. It wasn't a suggestion; it was a way of life. For that gift I am and will be eternally grateful. We are still avid readers, and we still love books.

We grew up in the sixties and seventies and didn't have the technologies that have become fixtures in our current lives. We had three television channels and one telephone...oh, the horror! What would today's kids do with that? I hope the same thing that we did; we made our own movies, our own fun, and used this thing called an imagination. Much of what we did came from something we read in a book. Yes, a book!

When we were very young, I can remember getting to go to the newly built public library in our community. My mom took the three of us, and we were so excited. I remember getting to go to the counter where the librarian handed me a card with my name on it—wow, my very own library card! I got to check out *my* stack of books and use *my* card. I felt so proud and so big! My sisters had their stacks, and off we went, anxiously waiting to get home to our books and read. It's funny, but I can still remember the smell of that library and how intently I watched the librarian stamp the return date on the card. The whole idea of the library was a thrill!

But...it didn't stop there! We didn't get to read just what we wanted; we also had to read something else. My dad came home with the evening newspaper, and we were expected to read current events to gain an understanding of what was going on in the world around us. So we became familiar with news, sports, arts, entertainment, and human interest stories. I didn't realize it then, but my parents were trying to create three well-rounded daughters who were also well versed in many areas, and it was done through being well read. I appreciate that atmosphere of learning my parents created for us. We carried on the tradition with our own kids too.

I'm not saying that reading is the only thing that shapes a child, but it does open one's eyes to the world created by others through words. Words are important! God spoke the world into existence by using words. Words are a creative force and can be used to harm or heal, build up or tear down.

Words create a visual. If someone says *newspaper*, I can envision my parents reading and their three girls sprawled out on the living room floor reading too. Someone can say a word, and a memory surfaces and evokes emotion. I can hear the words *hot bread*, and immediately I picture Grandma's kitchen table covered with her fresh baked rolls. I can still remember the smell. Words can stimulate our senses—they are that powerful.

God gave us words, and He also gave us a book. The Bible is our book, our standard, our history, and our hope. Where would we be without it, and, most importantly, *who* would we be without it? His book explains yesterday, graces today, and hopes for a tomorrow. It gives us an experience no other book can...it doesn't have an ending. No book can promise a forever or a real *happily-ever-after*. No author has written *that* story, and no library has housed *that* copy. There is only one—one story, one Savior, one cross, and one love...all in just one book.

I can remember three special books that my sisters and I carried every Sunday. Mine was white leather, and it zipped with a cross zipper pull and had my name in gold on the front cover. I remember how I felt when I got that book. It felt different than when I got that library card. What I got from library books were good stories, but what I got from that little white Bible was *the* story and...there was no return date stamped on the card.

MY PSALM

W E ARE OFTEN reminded of our need to be thankful, and I hope that message has come through loud and clear. We *do* need to be thankful and, moreover, to be thankful to God for all He has blessed us with. I believe that we all think of people and things to be thankful for, but what about the One? For me, as I sit in my office today, I can honestly say that *my cup runneth over.* I can list things, people, and experiences and find myself amazed at God's goodness and provision, but when I think of Him, just Him, I stand…simply in awe. When all is said and done, it's really all about Him.

To my heavenly Father, I say thank You. If my heart could only articulate what is felt with those two words. How can *thank You* even begin to cover it? Lord, You found me; what more could You offer? *Salvation alone would be enough, eternity with You is enough, but Your love wouldn't stop there.*

You stay with me every minute of every day as You hold my hand, my dreams, my fears, and, most of all, my heart. You handle that heart with the utmost care and with love that is tender and merciful. *This heart has been broken, but You have always been there to listen to it cry, and then You mend its bruised and torn places.*

You've given me "beauty for ashes," asking so little in return. When I've ignored You or been too busy, You've waited to hear my voice. When I call on You, I'm invited to see the beauty You unfold before me…so undeserving am I.

I've stumbled, I've fallen, and I've tried it my way, but mercy kept me until I finally figured out that Your way was always best. My long-suffering Father, You are so gracious with one like me. Your love chases me and is determined when I'm on shaky ground.

You offer Your *shalom* in times of confusion and indecision. You are the *Rock that is higher than I*—my shelter, safe place, and deliverer, my Lord in the midnights and the mornings. I hang my head in silent humility, in childlike wonder, in utter amazement that I heard the glorious gospel and that now heaven is mine—You are mine.

To the "glory and the lifter of my head," my words seem insufficient in the face of Your all-sufficiency. Only in You do I find the One who purposed my completion. Your steadfast love never ceases, and my love for You shall never cease as well! I love You with my life.

I will come home to You one day and lay my crown at Your feet—I dream of this day, but until then, I will live for the thought of it and for the thought of You, my Father—yes, I am thankful.

ACKNOWLEDGMENTS

THERE ARE SO many people to thank for making this life-long dream a reality. I remember hearing someone give an acceptance speech and stating, "There just aren't enough words for 'thank you,' are there?" I could not agree more! To say "thank you" cannot possibly begin to express the depths of gratitude that I feel in my heart…but I'll give it a try!

To my husband and best pal—thank you for continuing to encourage me in more ways than I can count. You have been a source of inspiration, and I've learned more by watching and *reading* you than anyone else I know. You always quote the line from *Lonesome Dove* and tell me, "It's been a party." It has been a party for sure—sometimes a surprise party, but a party nonetheless! When all is said and done, I wouldn't have it any other way.

To my Ashton and Austin—through the both of you I've gained an understanding of how God loves His children. You've been a point of reference countless times for that, as well as my teachers in many other ways. I cannot begin to express my heart in just a few sentences…you are my heaven on earth.

To the wonderful team at Charisma House—thank you for taking a chance by giving me one. Your kindness, patience, and understanding with this first-timer has been unparalleled. A million thank-yous to each and every one of you who was involved with this project.

To Andrea Lutchman—only you and I know there would not be a book without a YOU! Your tireless devotion and countless hours made this happen, not to mention your "to do" lists for me! Thank you for keeping me on task, being my dear friend, and for always saving me (especially with the Sonic Diet Cokes!).

To Sheila Withum—you were the lifesaver when I was drowning in a sea of notebooks with no idea what I was doing! You are amazing! Thank you for taking on this project and doing what you said you would: "Push me across the finish line!" Most of all, thank you for being my dear friend all these years.

To my parents, Oscar and Joann Askoff—you have given me a history that I treasure and a foundation of love that is unshakable. What I've drawn from both of you is matchless. Thank you for every moment of every year and for every time you said, "I'll be there in fifteen minutes!"

To Julie and Jenny—you're more than sisters; you are my best friends, and we have the history to prove it. Thank you being so wonderful and for absolutely everything (and only you know what that involves!). Plus, thanks for making me an aunt to your amazing kids—it's my second favorite title after Mom!

To more of my beloved family—my mother-in-law, Ellen Parsley, and my late father-in-law, James Parsley; my late sister-in-law, Debbie; and my nieces, my nephews, and my great-nieces: Amy, Matt, Jillian, Jared, Daniel, Ryan, Andrew, Jordan, Ava, and Lillian. I have learned so much about love, about life, about God, and about joy from all of you, and I am beyond blessed at the very thought of each of you.

To Sandy, Daisy, Tweet, Kate, and Jan—thank you for the all the times that you encouraged me to write through your words, your tears, your cheers, and your sincere friendship. I'll always remember it…always.

To my other extended families: World Harvest Church staff and congregation, *Joni's Journal*, and Breakthrough—what a blessing! Your encouragement has meant the world to me, and you kept me going *and* reaching! What an inspiration you are!

There is not enough space to thank so many others who've made a difference in my life and been the brightly colored hues in my tapestry of faith. I know and, moreover, God knows.

NOTES

Epigraph

1. "Tapestry" by Carole King, copyright © 1971, copyright management Colgems EM Music, Inc. Print license requested from Hal Leonard Corporation.

Part 1
Mirrored Image—Personal Growth

1. John Greenleaf Whittier, "Raphael," in *Poems of John Greenleaf Whittier* (Boston: James R. Osgood and Company, 1878), 131. Viewed at Google Books.

Lean On

1. "Leaning on the Everlasting Arms" by Elisha A. Hoffman. Public domain.

Just Keep Pedaling

1. Walt Whitman, "O Captain! My Captain," in *Leaves of Grass* (n.p.: Mundus Publishing, 1950). Viewed at Google Books.

Part 2
Life Support—Encouragement

1. As quoted in Charles Noel Douglas, compiler, *Forty Thousand Quotations* (London: George G. Harrap and Company, Ltd., 1904), 970. Viewed at Google Books.
2. "What a Friend We Have in Jesus" by Joseph M. Scriven. Public domain.

Extravagant Love

1. *Merriam-Webster's Collegiate Dictionary*, 11th ed. (Springfield, MA: Merriam-Webster, Inc., 2003), s.v. "extravagant."

GO, TELL IT FROM THE VALLEY

1. "Go, Tell It on the Mountain" by John W. Work Jr. Public domain.

SMILES

1. BrainyQuote.com, "Anne Morrow Lindbergh Quotes," http://www.brainyquote.com/quotes/authors/a/anne_morrow_lindbergh.html (accessed November 1, 2013).

PART 3
REASONS FOR THE SEASONS—CHANGE

1. Robert Frost, "Nothing Gold Can Stay," in *The Poetry of Robert Frost*, ed. Edward Connery Lathem (New York: Henry Holt and Company, 1969), 222–223. Viewed at Google Books.

AN EYE-DEFINING MOMENT

1. "Through It All" by Andrae Crouch. Copyright © 1971 Manna Music, Inc. Print license requested from ClearBox Rights, LLC.

PART 4
STATE OF MIND—THOUGHTS AND OPINIONS

1. As quoted in *Words of Wisdom*, ed. William Safire and Leonard Safire (New York: Simon and Schuster, 1989), 320. Viewed at Google Books.

LOST ART

1. Andrea Shea, "Facebook Envy: How the Social Network Affects Our Self-Esteem," WBUR.org, February 20, 2013, http://www.wbur.org/2013/02/20/facebook-perfection (accessed October 8, 2013).

PLATFORMS AND SOAPBOXES

1. Dr. Wilda, "Two Studies: Social Media and Social Dysfunction" (blog), April 13, 2013, http://drwilda.com/

2013/04/13/two-studies-social-media-and-social
-dysfunction/ (accessed October 8, 2013).

2. ThinkExist.com, "Ralph Waldo Emerson Quotes,"
http://thinkexist.com/quotation/people_do_not_seem_
to_realize_that_their_opinion/14513.html (accessed
October 8, 2013).

3. *New York Times Magazine*, "A Dramatic Shut-In,"
March 26, 2006, http://www.nytimes.com/2006/03/26/
magazine/326greenberg.html (accessed October 8,
2013).

Silence Is Golden

1. "The Solid Rock" by Edward Mote. Public domain.
2. "Rock of Ages" by Augustus M. Toplady. Public domain.

Part 5
Colorful Characters—Family, Motherhood, Relationships

1. As quoted in Tina L. Register, "Maya Angelou," African
American Literature Author Project, July 18, 2012, core
.ecu.edu/engl/deenas/africanamerican/MAYA%20
ANGELOU.doc (accessed October 8, 2013).

Something's Missing

1. Hannah Hurnard, *Hinds' Feet on High Places* (Radford,
VA: Wilder Publications, 2012). Originally published
1955.

Part 6
Built for the Battle—Struggles and Hardships

1. Helen Keller, "Part 1: Optimism Within," in *Optimism:
An Essay by Helen Keller* (N.p: Special Edition Books).
Viewed at Google Books.

Life, Interrupted

1. "Fix You" by Guy Rupert Berryman, Christopher
Anthony John Martin, Jonathan Mark Buckland, and

William Champion. Copyright Universal Music. Print license requested.

UNBROKEN

1. "The Solid Rock" by Edward Mote. Public domain.

THE ONE THING

1. Brennan Manning, *Ruthless Trust* (New York: Harper-Collins, 2009).

PART 7
CAREFUL CONSIDERATIONS—
REFLECTIONS AND MEDITATIONS

1. As quoted in John Maxwell, *The 15 Invaluable Laws of Growth* (New York: Hatchette Digital, Inc., 2012). Viewed at Google Books.

RANDOM THOUGHTS FROM THE STORAGE ROOM

1. "The Way We Were" by Marvin Hamlisch. Copyright EMI Music Publishing, Universal Music Publishing Group. Print license requested.

ESSENTIAL THINGS

1. Max Ehrmann, "Desiderata," copyright © 1927, renewed 1954. Permission requested.